D1691010

ULRICH DERNBACH'S
# Petrified Forests

*The World's 31 Most Beautiful Petrified Forests*

Authors: Rafael Herbst - Walter Jung - Alfred Selmeier - Friedemann Schaarschmidt - Evagelos Velitzelos - Ulrich Dernbach

Photographers: Kurt Noll - Robert Noll

## D'ORO

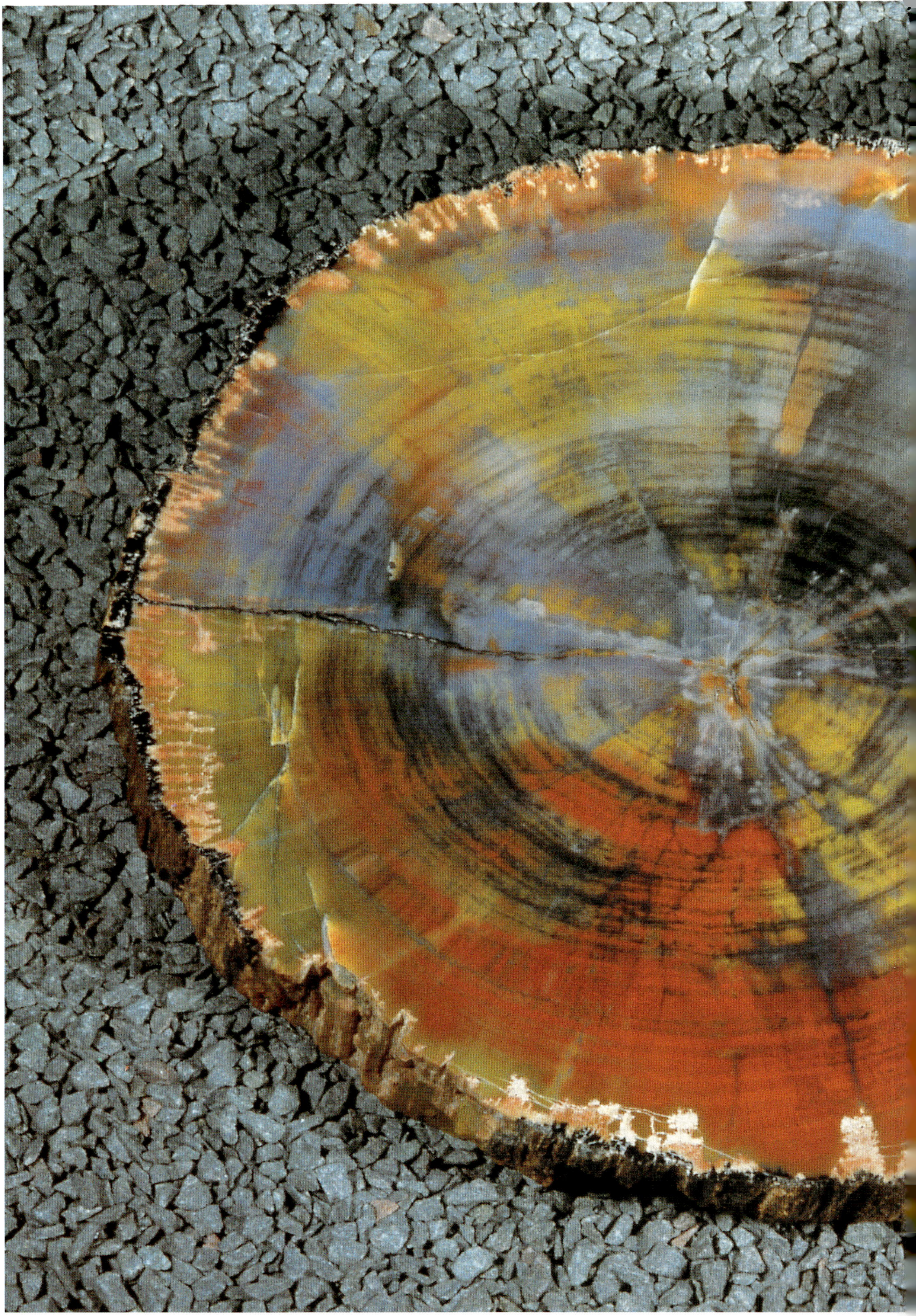

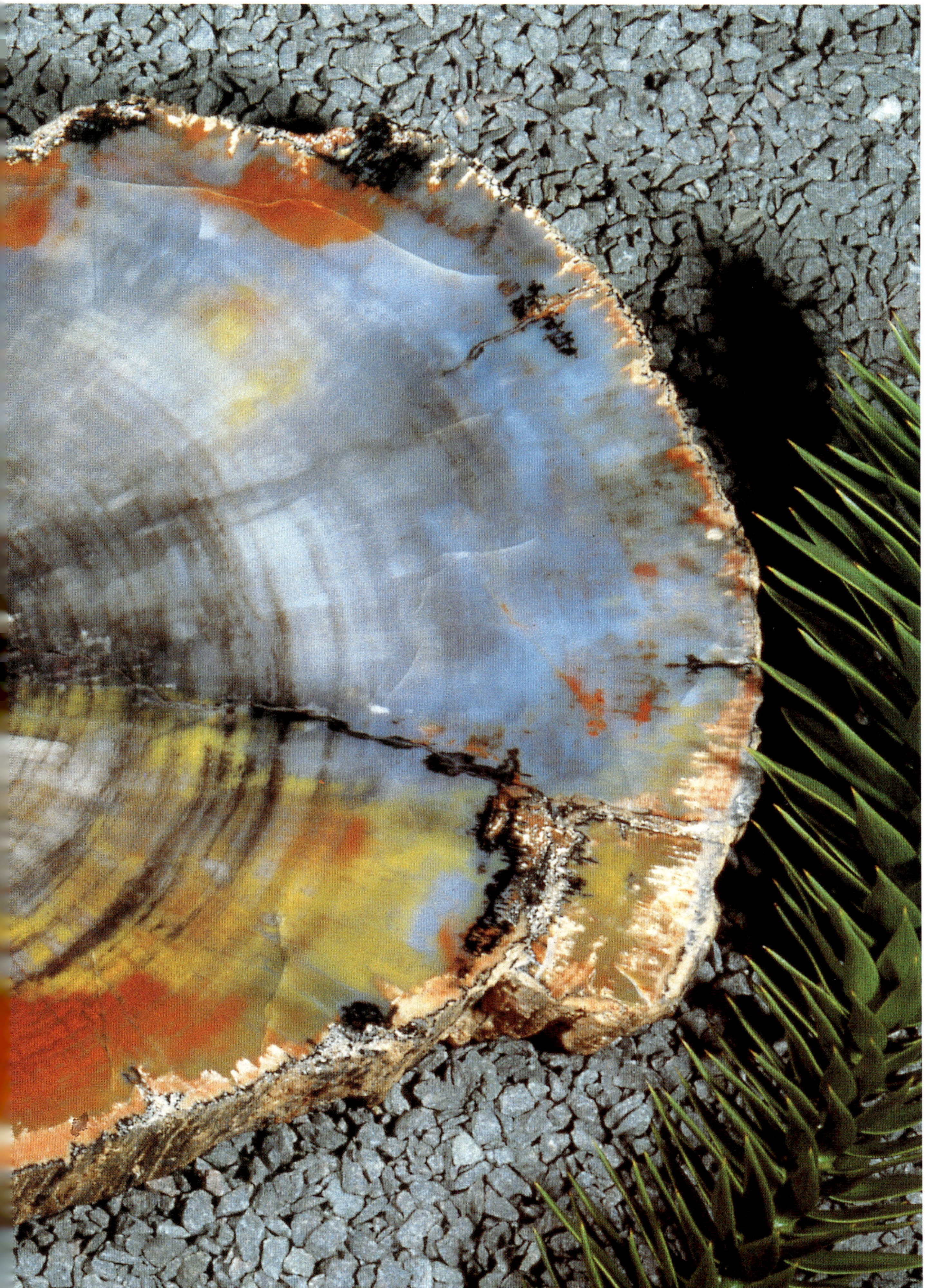

This book is dedicated to my dear wife. She was the unwavering companion at my side, patiently enduring the many vicissitudes of our travels. Her conciliatory manner and her famous "working dinners" invariably created a pleasant atmosphere at every meeting.

We extend our thanks to the authors of the scientific articles in this book: Prof. Rafael Herbst, Prof. Walter Jung, Prof. Friedemann Schaarschmidt, Prof. Alfred Selmeier and Prof. Evagelos Velitzelos.

We are grateful to our photographers, Kurt Noll and Robert Noll, whose artistiry and technical expertise made these gorgeous photos possible.

Many thanks to Eike Pätz, Henri Gielen, Dr. Guanghua Lin, Mr. and Mrs. Ray, Rüdiger Hesse and Ben Macray for their travel reports, all of whom contributed to the success of this book.

We thank Prof. Dietrich Herm, director of the Bavarian State Collection of Palaeontology and Historical Geology in Munich, for his generous loan of numerous specimens.

We would like to thank Prof. Steiringer, director of the Senckenberg Museum of Natural History and Research Institute in Frankfurt, for his permission to print illustration of *Cycadeoidea*.

Thanks to Mr. L. Kunzmann at the State Museum of Mineralogy and Geology in Dresden for preparing a photograph of *Raumeria*.

We thank Dr. Rößler, director of the Natural History Museum in Chemnitz, for his permission to take photographs inside the museum.

We especially want to thank Ali Iper and his son Bülent for their invitation to Ankara and for their hospitality.

Mr. Fremder, Hans Klein and Herbert Schmidt provided us with generous access to specimens and photographs.

Scientific information contributed by Giovanni Zingo, Kurt Balzer and Kurt Fritzsche added to the success of the volume. Our thanks go to each of those gentlemen.

Numerous friends guided us and provided us with valuable information during our visits to the various petrified forests. We'd like to thank Bill Branson, Dennis Murphy, Dan Riegel, Bill Rose, Ralph Thompson and Bob Whitmore in the U.S.A., Segundo and his family in Argentina, Decio Freitas in Brazil, and Mary White, Norman Donpon, Rod Hewer and Ron Smythe in Australia.

Gabriele Stachow, Julia Richter and Dr. Forster helped in the book's production, Howard Fine translated the texts into English.

Dörte and Ulrich Dernbach

# Contents

Preface ..................................................................................................................8

Imprint ..................................................................................................................9

*Time Table - The Evolution of Plants and Trees* ..................................................10

*Discovery Sites of Petrified Woods* ....................................................................12

*The World's 31 Most Beautiful Petrified Forests*

**NORTH AMERICA**

COLORADO, Florissant Fossil Beds Petrified Forest ............................................20

OREGON, The Deschutes ....................................................................................22

OREGON, Stinkingwater ......................................................................................24

OREGON, McDermitt ..........................................................................................26

UTAH, The Petrified Forests ................................................................................28

WYOMING, Blue Forest ......................................................................................32

WYOMING, Yellowstone National Park ..............................................................36

WASHINGTON, Ginkgo Petrified Forest ..............................................................42

CALIFORNIA, The Petrified Forest of Calistoga ..................................................46

NEVADA, Virgin Valley Petrified Forest ..............................................................50

ARIZONA, The Petrified Forest of Arizona ..........................................................56

**SOUTH AMERICA**

ARGENTINA, The Petrified Forests of Patagonia ................................................64

ARGENTINA, José Ormaechea Petrified Forest ..................................................68

ARGENTINA, Szlapelis Petrified Forest ..............................................................72

BRAZIL, The Petrified Forest of Sao Pedro do Sul ..............................................74

BRAZIL, Araguaina Petrified Forest ....................................................................78

**AFRICA**

EGYPT, The Petrified Forest of Cairo ..................................................................82

NAMIBIA, The Petrified Forest of Namibia ..........................................................84

ZIMBABWE, The Petrified Forest of Zimbabwe ..................................................86

MADAGASCAR, The Petrified Forest of Madagascar ..........................................90

*AUSTRALIA*

QUEENSLAND, The Petrified Forest of Queensland ..................................................................96

TASMANIA, The Petrified Forest of Tasmania .......................................................................100

*NEW ZEALAND*

NEW ZEALAND, The Petrified Forest of New Zealand ...........................................................104

*ASIA*

CHINA, The Petrified Forest of Xinjiang ................................................................................106

*EUROPE*

BELGIUM, The Petrified Forest of La Calamine .....................................................................108

GERMANY, The Petrified Forest of Chemnitz .......................................................................110

CZECH REPUBLIC, The Petrified Forest of Nová Paka ...........................................................116

GREECE, The Petrified Forest of Lesbos ...............................................................................118

GREECE, The Petrified Forest of Lemnos ..............................................................................124

TURKEY, The Petrified Forest of Istanbul .............................................................................126

TURKEY, The Petrified Forest of Ankara ..............................................................................130

*The Tree* ............................................................................................................................134

*Identification of Petrified Wood Made Easy* .....................................................................136

*Tree Ferns - Past and Present* ...........................................................................................148

*Ferns, Cycads, or What?* ...................................................................................................156

*Cycadophytes - Plant Relics from the Days of the Dinosaurs* ...........................................160

*Pentoxylon from Gondwana* ............................................................................................168

*Araucarias - Wanderers Between North and South* ........................................................170

*The Ginkgo - Forever Green* .............................................................................................176

Bibliography ........................................................................................................................182

Glossary ..............................................................................................................................184

The Authors ........................................................................................................................186

# *Preface*

**Ulrich Dernbach**

Naturally, I'm well aware that a book about the world's petrified forests can never claim to be complete. Enormous and still unexplored areas in South America and Asia may well contain as yet undiscovered petrified forests. Nevertheless, I believe that this book has succeeded in its goal of surveying the world's most important and most attractive discovery sites.

Petrified wood has been found at a great many sites all over the world. I personally know of several dozen sites in Germany alone where petrified wood can be found in fields or gravel beds. But do these sites deserve to be classed as petrified "forests"? Naturally not!

Experts use the term "petrified forest" to describe a site where large quantities of silicified trees can be found at the place where they once grew (autochthonous). Another criterion is the stratified structure of herbs, bushes and several layers of trees. If one were to use this strict definition of the term, only a handful of "true" petrified forests could be discussed in this book. We have therefore chosen to extend the scope of the term "petrified forest" to include non-autochthonous forests; I also report on famous sites where one must now dig to find silicified tree trunks and branches, although not long ago at many of these sites, enormous quantities of petrified wood still lay strewn upon the earth's surface.

It was not my intention to write a technical, scientific tome. Rather, the present volume is meant as a combination of a lavishly illustrated picture-book and a reference guide featuring scientifically accurate reports by renowned palaeobotanists.

If, after reading this book, the reader finds it easier to identify specimens of petrified wood, and if he or she should feel motivated to visit one or another of the forests described within it, then this book shall have fulfilled its purpose.

# Imprint

**Petrified Forests**
*The World's 31 Most Beautiful Petrified Forests.*

**D'ORO-Verlag**
Germany 1996

Schlehenweg 2
D-64646 Heppenheim
Tel.: 06252/5661
Fax: 06252/68587

Idea:
Dörte and Ulrich Dernbach

Artistic Conception:
Herbert Herzog, Bonn

Graphic Design:
Manfred Langer, Bonn

Photos:
Except where credited otherwise, all photos in the travel reports were taken by Ulrich Dernbach.

Except where credited otherwise, Kurt Noll and Robert Noll prepared the specimens and took the photographs and microscopic photographs of petrified woods.

Except where credited otherwise, all depicted specimens are from the collection of Ulrich Dernbach.

Translation:
Howard Fine, Munich

Lithography:
PPP Preprint Partner, Bonn

Printing:
Druckerei Läufer, Mannheim

ISBN 3-932181-02-6

Produced in Germany

Rights:
"Petrified Forests" and all of its texts and illustrations are protected by copyright. Any use thereof except within the narrow limits specified by copyright laws without permission of the publishers is prohibited and punishable.

| Geological Age | Formation | | Petrified Forests... |
|---|---|---|---|
| Cenozoic | Quaternary | | e.g., Trunks in Chalk Sinter |
| | | 1.7 million years ago | |
| | Tertiary | | **Florissant**, Colorado, USA; **Vantage**, Washington, USA; **Deschutes**, Oregon, USA; **McDermitt**, Oregon, USA; **Virgin Valley**, Nevada, USA; **Blue Forest**, Wyoming, USA; **Yellowstone National Park**, Wyoming, USA; **Calistoga**, California, USA; **Rio Cauca**, Colombia; **José Ormaechea**, Argentina; **Szlapelis**, Argentina; **Mikófälva**, Hungary; **Lesbos and Lemno**, Greece; **Zuri-Soddi**, Sardinia; **Ankara**, Turkey; **Istanbul**, Turkey; **Cairo**, Egypt; **Pondicherry**, India; **Deccan Intertrappean**, India; **Mandalay**, Myanmar; **Hubei Province**, China; **Mawaki**, Japan |
| | | 65 | |
| Mesozoic | Cretaceous | | **La Calamine**, Belgium; **Port Edward**, South Africa; **Lhasa**, Tibet |
| | | 145 | |
| | Jurassic | | **Cerro Cuadrado**, Argentina; **Xinjiang**, China; **New Zealand**; **Queensland**, Australia; **Tasmania**, Australia |
| | | 210 | |
| | Triassic | | **Arizona**, USA; **Utah**, USA; **Sao Pedro do Sul**, Brazil; **Khorixas**, Namibia; **Zimbabwe**; **Madagascar** |
| | | 245 | |
| Palaeozoic | Permian | | **Araguaina**, Brazil; **Chemnitz**, Germany; **Nová Paka**, Czech Republic; **New Caledonia** |
| | | 290 | |
| | Carboniferous | | e.g., *Stigmaria* roots |
| | | 360 | |
| | Devonian | | **Gilboa, New York**, USA |
| | | 410 | |
| | Silurian | | no forests |
| | | 440 | |
| | Ordovician | | no forests |
| | | 510 | |
| | Cambrian | | no forests |
| | | 570 | |
| Archaic | Precambrian | | no forests |
| | | 4600 | |

* Dates shown in millions of years before the present day

# ... and Their Trees

**Present-day Forests**

**Palms
Deciduous Trees
Modern Needle-bearing Trees**

fan palm (Palmacites)

amber tree (Liquidambar)

water pine (Glyptostrobus)

**First Deciduous Trees
Needle-bearing Trees
Cycadophytes
Ginkgophytes
Tree Ferns**

cycadophyte (Cycadeoidea)

tree fern (Tempskya)

**Ancient Needle-bearing Trees
Ginkgophytes
Cycadophytes
Later Seed Ferns
Tree Ferns**

needle-bearing tree (Pararaucaria)

Ginkgo

cycadophyte (Nilssonia)

**First Needle-bearing Trees
Cordaites
Early Seed Ferns
Tree Ferns
*Sigillaria* and *Lepidodendron* Trees
Calamites**

tree fern (Asterotheca)

seed fern (Glossopteris)

calamite (Annularia)

**First "Petrified Forest"**

sigillaria (Sigillaria)

primordial seed plant (Callixylon)

primordial land plant (Aglaophyton)

**Bacteria and Algae**

"alga" stromatolite (Stromatolith)

**No Organisms At First**

# Discovery Sites of Petrified Woods

**Alfred Selmeier**

Although the following compilation does not claim to be exhaustive, when considered as a complement to U. Dernbach's descriptions of 31 locations, it does provide a general overview of the world's most significant discovery sites for petrified woods. Some 1,000 xylem-anatomical original publications on petrified woods were individually examined and geographically grouped. Depending on the number of verified discovery sites per continent or region, it was sometimes impossible to mention all of them in the following list. This compilation focuses exclusively on sites where petrified woods have been found; it does not include sites where lignites have been discovered.

## North America

Petrified woods have been found in every state of the United States and in each of Canada's provinces. Elsewhere in this book, U. Dernbach reports on his personal visits to eleven extensive petrified forests in North America. Most of these sites are located in the western part of the continent in Washington, Oregon, Wyoming, California, Nevada (ill.1.2), Utah, Colorado and Arizona. Many are well-known petrified forests and/or national parks, some of which are frequently visited by tourists. On the eastern side of the continent, in the Catskill Mountains not far from Albany, New York, a petrified forest was discovered at Gilboa, New York in 1869. Trunks of *Psaronius* and *Lyginodendron* have been found in this Lower Devonian forest.

Ill. 1.1
Tertiary palm,
Texas

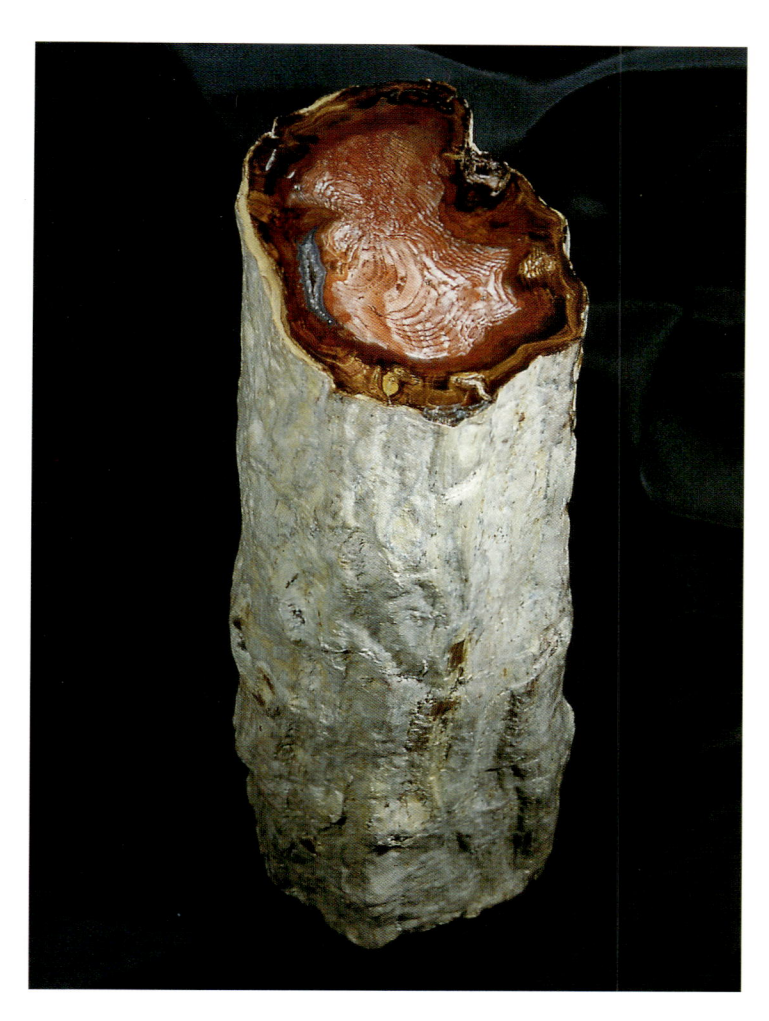

Ill. 1.2 Tertiary conifer, Nevada

Numerous specimens of petrified woods have also been found in the Canadian arctic. A few discovery sites on or near the 72nd parallel include Amund Ringnes Island, Ellesmere Island and Mackenzie King Island. Additional specimens have also been found in the Mackenzie River region and on Banks Island. A sizeable quantity of petrified coniferous driftwood has been recovered from Lower Cretaceous sediments in Sverdrup Basin. Upper Cretaceous petrifications in the Taxodiaceae family have been described from the region around Drumheller, Alberta.

## Central America

H.R.Göppert (1835) mentions more than 200 specimens of petrified wood found in Cretaceous formations on Antigua Island. Woods from many parts of the Caribbean have found their way into European collections. J.Felix (1882, 1883) was the first researcher to examine the anatomy of thin sections prepared from West Indian petrified specimens. He identified these specimens as the remains of deciduous trees and palms. Individual discoveries in Mexico, Cuba and the northern part of the Dominican Republic (Jarabacoa) have also been reported, but on the whole, attractive sites that truly merit the appellation "petrified forests" are lacking in Central America.

## South America

The petrified araucaria forest of Cerro Cuadrado in Patagonia, southern Argentina, numbers among the world's largest petrified forests. Compared to the well-known Petrified Forest in Arizona, Cerro Cuadrado is much more primeval, harsher, and considerably less easily accessible. In his fascinating and lavishly illustrated book *Araucaria*, U. Dernbach introduced Cerro Cuadrado Petrified Forest to the world and featured it in a commensurably impressive publication able to do full justice to this forest's major palaeontological significance.

Many scientific publications have reported on successful efforts to investigate the anatomy and determine the identity of petrified woods discovered in the famous national parks. Descriptive brochures, together with reconstructions of the landscape and its vegetation labeled with the names of the needle-bearing or deciduous trees that once grew at these sites, are available for use by visitors to these parks.

Current scientific research into North American petrified woods focuses on Cretaceous and Lower Tertiary specimens. Some of the latest field expeditions searched for remains of pre-Tertiary woods, i.e., specimens which would represent early stages or precursors in the evolutionary ancestry of deciduous trees. Hundreds of Cretaceous petrified woods recovered from sites in California are providing valuable information into the basic structural patterns of primordial deciduous plants; these specimens include slender sapling trunks, twigs and roots (V.M. Page).

Specimens of petrified woods from deciduous Upper Cretaceous to Eocene trees, many of which display interesting woody structures, have recently been found in eastern Oregon, southeastern Texas (ill. 1.1), Louisiana, and Big Bend National Park in Texas.

Elsewhere in this book, U.Dernbach describes his personal visits to all other major petrified forests of South America. These sites are located in Brazil (Araguaina, Sao Pedro do Sul) and Argentina (Cerro Cuadrado, José Ormaechea [ill. 1.3], Szlapelis). Compared to the relatively large number of sites known in North America,

Ill. 1.3
Tertiary petrified forest, Argentina

Ill. 1.5
Triassic *Dadoxylon*, Germany

Europa, Africa and Asia, the continent of South America seems to feature petrified woods at only a relatively few sites. Except for the aforementioned petrified forests, hardly any other locations are even mentioned in the literature. Charles Darwin (1809-1882) was very likely the first scientist to report on South American petrified woods; his discussion describes the numerous silicified trunks found at Aspallata Pass in northern Chile. H.Conwentz describes Tertiary specimens from Rio Negro Province in Argentina. Petrified woods which have been subjected to detailed xylem-anatomical identification derive from Tertiary layers in Columbia, from Tertiary sites in Peru and Patagonia (Cerro Dorotea, Magellan Province), from Permian Irati layers near Rio Claro, Sao Paulo, from the Andes at Aconcagua in Chile, and elsewhere. Petrified woods of the *Rhexoxylon* type have been found in the Ischigualasto region of northwestern Argentina; these Tertiary specimens are first mentioned in literature published in 1961. Quiriquina Island, six miles (10 km) northwest of Talcahuano, Chile, has yielded a number of Upper Cretaceous and Tertiary specimens derived from conifers and deciduous trees. A Japanese team recently undertook several expeditions to southern Chile. This team discovered more than 200 petrified specimens of Tertiary woods including woods from the deciduous genera *Nothofagus* (southern beech), *Fagus* (beech) and *Laurus* (laurel). The discovery site, which is called Cerro Dorotea, features a series of 1,640-foot-tall (500-meter-tall) hills located 11 miles (18 km) north-northeast of Puerto Natales, Chile at 52° South latitude. Estancia Filaret on Fuego Island is located some 25 miles (40 km) south of Cullen; numerous petrified woods have recently been found here as well. T.G.

Halle mentions the discovery of *Dadoxylon* wood in Permian deposits on West Point Island (in the Falkland Islands, also known as Las Islas Malvinas).

# Europe

Elsewhere in this book U.Dernbach uses the term "petrified forest" in his descriptions of petrified trunks from Lesbos, Ankara, Istanbul, Chemnitz and La Calamine. Older literature likewise frequently refers to the Miocene forest at Zuri-Soddi, Cagliari Province, Sardinia as a "petrified forest." A significant European center for the collection and identification of petrified woods is the Laboratoire de Paléobotanique et Paléoécologie, Univérsité Paris 6, France. Founded by Prof. E.Boureau, this institution focuses its research on specimens of petrified woods recovered from French sites, although it has also published valuable information about specimens gathered in Southeast Asia, Africa and South America.

Petrified woods have been discovered at so many different European locations that only a selection of major sites can be offered here. Great Britain: Shetland and Orkney Islands, Hebrides, Firth of Forth, the coasts of Suffolk, Essex and Kent, Isle of Wight, and Hampshire Basin. Petrified trunks found at Lough Neagh, Ireland are mentioned in literature published in 1751. France: Massif Central, Puy-de-Dome, Cantal, l'Autun Basin, Paris Basin, Pays de Caux and Pas-de-Calais. Germany: debris and pyrite woods in the glaciated area of northern Germany, keuper woods in southern Thuringia, Franconia (ill. 1.4, 1.5) and Baden-Württemberg, Palaeozoic woods in the Saar and Nahe Valleys, and numerous deposits of Tertiary driftwood in the northern alpine Molasse Basin of Bavaria. In addition, large amounts of petrified woods have also been recovered from sites in Austria and Switzerland (Delsberger Basin), Hungary (Tokaj-Eperjeser Mountains), Romania and the Czech Republic. Relatively few specimens have been found in Italy, Spain, Portugal and Poland. Finally, a few Russian discovery sites also deserve mention: Apscheron Peninsula, Kuznetsk Basin, Kazakhstan (93 miles/150 km) northeast of Karaganda, and the Kuvsk Region), as well as fossils found in Kamchatka.

## Iceland and Arctic Regions

In his *Flora Fossilis Arctica* (1868), O. Heer mentions fossilized woods found in the western part of the island "south of Paulaberg in Borgarfjord's Syssel." Additional specimens of petrified wood from needle-bearing and deciduous trees have been recovered from Tertiary layers at Tjörnes, Hrutagil near Fell (in northwestern Iceland), and at Lodmundarfjord (eastern Iceland). The specimens from Spitzbergen were first collected during the Torell Expedition of 1858. These are Palaeozoic woods from the region around Sassen Bay, as well as some Triassic gymnosperm wood from Eisfjord and Upper Jurassic woods from Green Harbor, Esmarks Glacier and Wimansberg. Petrified woods have been found and anatomically described from Tertiary layers at Lindsströmberg and Nordenskiöld and from the more easterly located island King Karl's Land. Additional specimens have been recovered from Franz Josef Land, Greenland (Myggbukta), and from other islands in the Arctic Ocean.

Ill. 1.7 Triassic *Woodworthia*, Zimbabwe, section with growth boundary

## Africa

Friedrich Hasselquist, a student of the great Swedish natural scientist Linné, collected petrified woods near Heliopolis in Egypt in 1750. A century later, F. Unger described Egyptian specimens as *Dadoxylon aegyptiacum*. All reports on travels undertaken by palaeontologists and geographers mention the "petrified forests" near Cairo and other deposits of petrified woods in the dry landscapes of North Africa. The trunks from Bir el Fahme near Cairo were originally between 33 and 92 feet (10 and 28 meters) long with diameters of up to 39.4 inches (one meter). Large petrified trunks from the desert regions of North Africa have frequently been carried to fireplaces or erected as landmarks atop elevated places in the terrain. Since these woods are rarely found in outcropping

Ill. 1.4 Triassic *Woodworthia*, Germany

Ill. 1.8
Triassic tree trunk, Namibia
Photo: Eike Pätz

layers, estimates of their geologic ages vary widely. (Denudation relics and secondary embedding after landslides in wadis further complicate the problem of determining their true ages.) According to German palaeontologists R.Kräusel and E.Stromer there are "no reliable reports" of vertically oriented (i.e., still standing) petrified trunks anywhere in Africa. Journals of expeditions, travelers' reports and palaeontological literature mention some 130 different African locations where petrified woods have been found. As personally observed during my own many-years-long residence in Egypt, again and again one can discover pieces of petrified wood strewn across barren and nearly plant-free landscapes. The following is an alphabetical listing of some countries where anatomically well-preserved petrified woods have been found: Algeria, Cameroon, Chad, Ethiopia, Ghana, Guinea, Kenya, Liberia, Libya, Mali, Mauritania, Morocco, Mozambique, Namibia (ill. 1.8), Niger, Senegal, Somalia, Sudan, Tunisia, Uganda, Zaire, Zimbabwe (ill. 1.6, 1.7). The majority of African specimens derive from deciduous flora, especially from genera like *Acacioxylon* and *Albizzioxylon* in the Mimosaceae family. Palaeontologists A.Chiarugi, R.Dechamps, J.P.Gros and J.-C.Koeniguer have worked with and anatomically identified many specimens of African petrified woods. An excellent standard text for the identification of Africa's petrified woods is R. Kräusel's treatment of 386 Egyptian petrified woods. R.Kräusel, a palaeobotanist and field scientist, also provides descriptions of petrified woods from South Africa. These specimens are highly interesting from an anatomical standpoint.

A transverse section of Mesozoic *Rhexoxylon* trunk discovered on Schlangenkopf Farm near Seeheim in the Keetmanshoo District shows centrifugally and centripetally developed woody wedges. Two additional attributes of this specimen are also worthy of note: it shows secondary growth of parenchyma and its wood is divided into separate wedges. Specimens of *Rhexoxylon* have also been found in Zimbabwe (Willoughby's Gwelo), in Cape Province (Aliwal North) and in Orange Free State (Fourie Farm, Steynspruit). More recent discoveries of this same genus have been made at sites in Australia, Tasmania, India and Argentina. Although in the past (1956) it was suspected that a relationship existed between *Rhexoxylon* and lianas, more recent research has shown that these unusual specimens in fact belong to a small group of Mesozoic seed ferns (Corystospermales).

Yet another site where silicified woods have been found is located near Port Edward in the eastern region of Cape Province (Pondoland). Numerous petrified tree trunks are deposited in sediments together with marine fauna (Umzamba Layers, Upper Senonian). The specimens are found along a stretch of steep coastline between the mouths of the Umzamba and Umtamvuna Rivers. Tidal action, working in concert with the erosive effects of surf along the high and low water lines, disinters the ancient trunks and contributes to their destruction and erosion. Many broken pieces of petrified trunk have been worn and smoothed by wave action to create rounded lumps of beach gravel. Because of the orientation in which these trunks are found, scientists believe that these trees originally grew farther inland, were deposited as driftwood on the coast, and were subsequently buried beside the bay together with marine sediments from the Cretaceous ocean. E.Mädel (1962) examined petrified woods which R. Kräusel (1954) brought back from his expedition to southern and southwestern Africa. Anatomical identification revealed that 51% of the specimens derived from gymnosperms and 49% from deciduous trees (especially from the Monimiaceae family, as well as some Euphorbiaceae). Arboreal Monimiaceae and Euphorbiaceae are still widely distributed throughout tropical regions today.

The western part of Madagascar is particularly rich in petrified woods. Some discovery sites on this large island lie between Mahajanga and Toliara, east of Maintirano, and near Morandava. Elsewhere in this book, U. Dernbach reports on his visits to "petrified forests" near Cairo, in Namibia and Zimbabwe.

# Asia

Extensive "petrified forests" such as can be admired in North and South America are not found in Asia. Thus far, scientists have recovered only relatively small collections of petrified wood.

Ill. 1.9
Geographers from Hubei University, Wuhan, China
Photo: A. Selmeier

Ill. 1.6
Triassic *Woodworthia*, Zimbabwe

## China and Tibet

D.Shuyion (1987) reported on a "petrified forest" near Beijing. Silicified woods have been found and identified (1984) in Cretaceous deposits in southern Xixang, near Lhasa in Tibet. A joint German-Chinese team collected petrified woods in the Jiaduo region north of Lhasa in 1983. Geographers from Hubei University in Wuhan have found a number of large petrified trunks in Tertiary sediments in the center of Hubei Province (1987); these specimens have since been identified as the remains of deciduous trees. Gymnosperm woods have recently been found in Cretaceous layers in Liaoning Province in northeastern China.

## India

The Birbal Sahni Institute of Paleobotany in Lucknow is the center of all palaeobotanical activities in Asia. Since 1952, that institute's journal "The Paleobotanist" has published numerous articles reporting on the collection of petrified woods. Over the past fifty years, the thorough anatomical examination of petrified specimens has shown that many different kinds of woods from both deciduous as well as needle-bearing trees deserve to be included in newly established taxa. Indian sites where petrified woods have been found include: Pondicherry (Cuddalore Series), Mandla District (Deccan Intertrappean Series), northwestern India (Assam, Nagaland), and Pliocene deposits in Mothala, Kutch District. Large petrifications from the Cuddalore Series can be admired at Tiruvakkarai Fossil Park.

Ill. 1.10
Tertiary oak, Australia

## Thailand, Cambodia

Petrified woods have been found along the shores of the Gulf of Thailand, in the vicinity of the city of Phayao in northwestern Thailand, and on the Khorat Plateau. At elevations of approximately 130 feet (40 m), and especially between Chwang and Thalaborivat, terraces along the Mekong River in Cambodia have yielded numerous specimens of petrified woods. The wood anatomy of fossil specimens from Thailand has been studied by the French scientists C.Vozenin-Serra and C. Privé-Gill. Petrified woods have also been found in Burma, now known as Myanmar. As early as 1800, M.Symes reported that "...the fossil wood of Burma has attracted the attention more than any other mineral substances." Specimens of 37 petrified Tertiary woods, collected during geological investigations along the Chindwinn River (a tributary of the Irrawaddy), have been identified as deriving from deciduous trees belonging to 14 different families. An apparently Mesozoic specimen of ginkgo wood was found in Quang-Nam Province. The Linh Plateau in southern Vietnam has yielded numerous specimens of Neogene angiosperm woods.

## Japan

As early as 1907, K. Reiss wrote a dissertation about the fossilized woods of Japan. S.Watari investigated Tertiary woody floras from the northern, western and central regions of Honshu; Y.Ogura and Shimakura reported on additional Miocene deposits in southern Hokkaido. More recently, M. Suzuki has been among the foremost researchers involved in the identification of newly discovered petrified woods. Several discovery sites deserve mention: central Japan (Kwanto Mountains, Ishikawa District), Noto Peninsula (Mawaki) in Honshu, Upper Cretaceous layers on Hokkaido, and Oligocene sediments on the southern island of Kyushu. A garden on the grounds of the Buddhist temple at Sojiji includes a monument built from 32 of the 72 petrified woods that have been

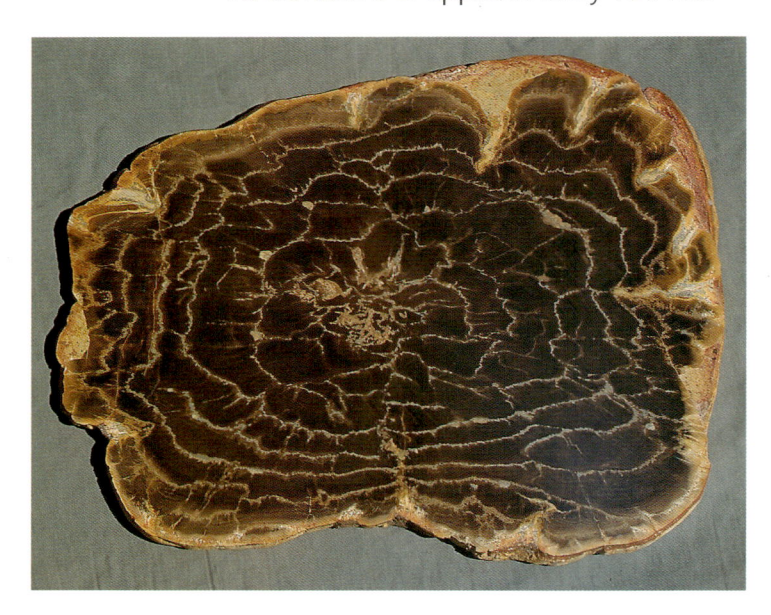

Ill. 1.12
Jurassic *Pentoxylon*, Australia

Ill. 1.11
Jurassic
Osmundaceae,
Australia

collected on Noto Peninsula in Nakaya and Nigoriike. The remains of Miocene tree trunks displayed here are dedicated to the memory of the victims of a catastrophic landslide that devastated the town of Nakaya.

## The Islands of Southeastern Asia

H. J. Goeppert first described petrified woods from Java in 1854. By the turn of the century, additional specimens had been discovered on Sumatra, Java, New Guinea, Timor and among the Philippine Islands. R. Kräusel launched a new era with his pioneering anatomical investigations of petrified woods (1922-1926). Dutch and German geologists collected an abundance of petrified woods on Dutch colonial islands. H.-J. Schweitzer worked with these materials and published his findings in a monograph (1958) in which he announced that he had identified some 250 different woods in the Dipterocarpaceae family; nearly one-third of all Indonesian fossilized woods belong to this family. Along with gymnosperm and palm woods, K. Kramer (1974) also discovered woods belonging to 16 other families of deciduous trees. Tertiary woods from southeastern Asia have been found on Borneo, Celebes, Timor, Seram, Obi, Talaud, New Guinea and elsewhere. Petrified woods are sometimes so common on Java and Sumatra that they have been used as gravel for building roads and railway lines. M. Salard examined the xylem anatomy of Palaeozoic woods from New Caledonia and determined that these specimens belong to the genus *Sahnioxylon* and to certain other genera.

# Australia and New Zealand

Elsewhere in this book, U. Dernbach reports in detail about discovery sites of petrified woods in Australia (Queensland and Tasmania) and New Zealand. A highly unusual "petrified forest" is visible in New Zealand only at ebb tide: it is located on the southeastern coast of South Island between the towns of Invercargill and Dunedin, along the shore of Curio Bay about 53 miles (85 km) south of Waikawa. Jurassic specimens found here are believed to be the remains of *Araucaria heterophylla*, the Norfolk Island pine.

# Antarctica

Because so many geological reports have been published about this continent and its petrified woods, it is difficult to determine which publication deserves the honor of being recognized as the earliest. There can be no doubt, however, that the Swedish South Pole Expedition of 1901-1903 was among the first field excursions to collect petrified specimens in Antarctica. W. Gotham investigated the anatomical characteristics of fossilized woods found on Seymour Island and on Snow Hill Island during that expedition. Antarctica's petrified woods are found in Permian, Mesozoic or Tertiary layers.

Permian silicified woods and their discovery sites: Transantarctic Mountains; northern and southern Victoria Land; and East Antarctica. Some discovery sites of Mesozoic woods: Beardmore Glacier Region and Fremouw Peak. The majority of Mesozoic woods have been found on the Antarctic Peninsula. E.Taylor reported on a specimen of trunk which appears similar to *Rhexoxylon*. Tertiary woods have been found on the Antarctic Peninsula and its neighboring islands, including Seymour Island, Snow Hill Island, King George Island, Livingstone Island. Edwards describes Tertiary coniferous woods found on the Kerguélen Islands (latitude 49° South). Southern beech (*Nothofagus*) is an interesting Tertiary wood found in the Antarctic.

# COLORADO

# Florissant Fossil Beds

Ulrich Dernbach

Did you know that one of the world's largest deposits of fossils is located high up in the Rocky Mountains of Colorado?

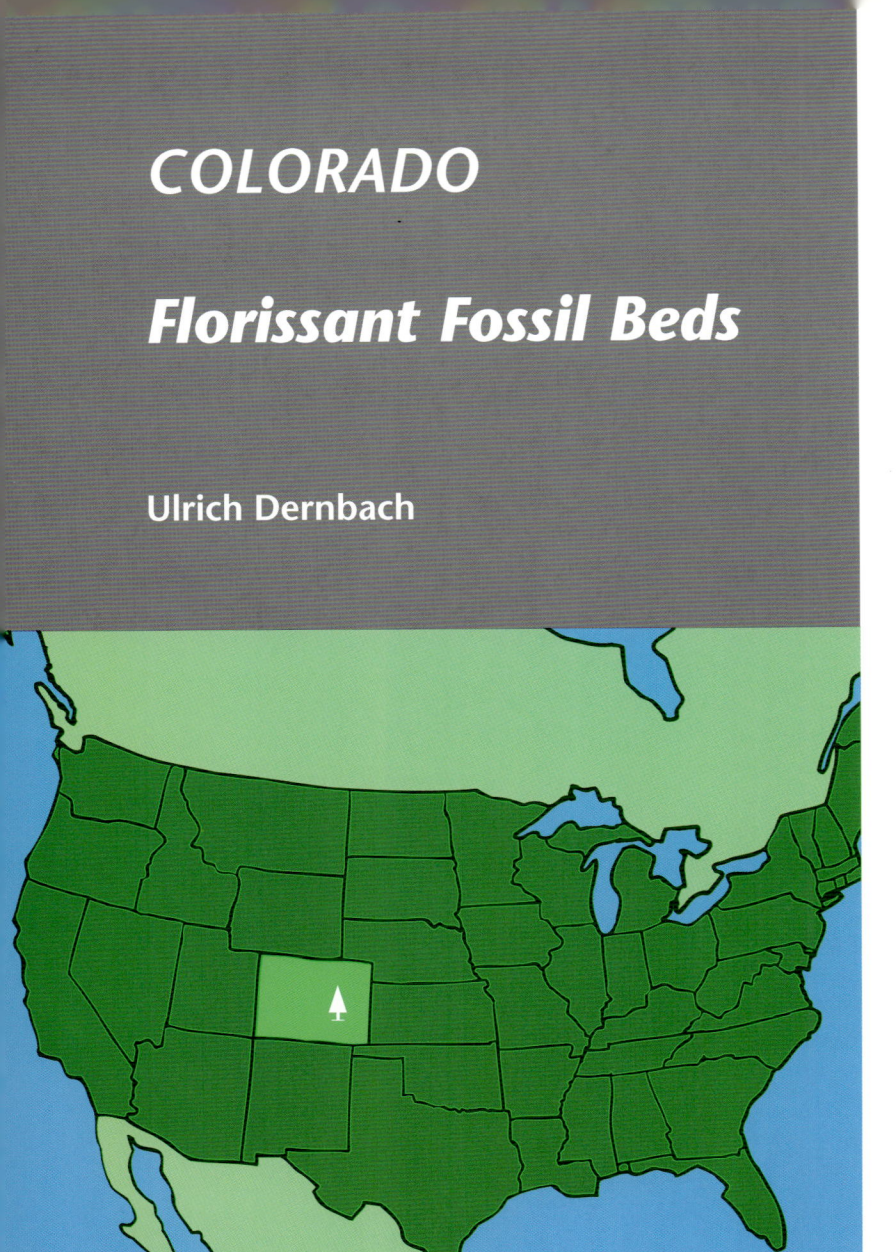

Experts estimate that fossil insects alone have yielded 1,200 different varieties. Fossils of fishes, birds, mammals and snakes are by no means seldom either. And as if that weren't wonder enough, the location also features petrified sequoia trunks - still standing erect - whose extraordinary girths and diameters are truly astonishing. Never before have I seen such colossal giants.

I'm pleased to reveal to you the name of this unique, Oligocene epoch (34 to 37 million year old) natural park: Florissant Fossil Beds.

**How to Get There**

Drive west from Colorado Springs for 30 miles (48 km) along Highway 24 until you reach Florissant, then turn left onto Route 1. This road will take you directly to Florissant Fossil Beds and into the petrified forest.

By the way: if you continue along Route 1 another 16 miles (26 km), you'll reach Cripple Creek, one of the oldest gold-digger's towns in the U.S.A. The mines around Cripple Creek continue to yield moderate amounts of gold even today. The town is definitely worth a visit, not only because of the good restaurants and plentiful gambling casinos.

Ill. 2.4  Sequoia slice

It's definitely worth your while to follow the footpath and enjoy the easy, one-mile (1.6-kilometer) hike through the park. As you stroll, you'll pass no fewer than seven sites where these enormous and impressive relics from the past are still standing upright (ill 2.1, 2.2). Together with a park ranger, I measured the largest petrified tree stump: without exaggeration, our honest tape measure told us that this petrified giant was a colossal 48 feet (14.6 m) in circumference and had an almost unimaginable diameter of 15.5 feet (4.7 m) (ill. 2.3).

Ill. 2.1

Ill. 2.2

Ill. 2.3

### The Petrified Forest at Florissant

Situated at an altitude of 9,200 feet (2,800 m), Florissant Petrified Forest is very likely the world's highest-altitude petrified forest.

About 35 million years ago, when the climate in this region was considerably warmer than it is today, extensive forests of hickory, beech, maple, oak, walnut, fir, cedar and sequoia trees flourished here. Thus far, however, no one has solved the riddle of why only petrified sequoia trunks and no other type of tree trunks have been found in this park (ill. 2.4).

# OREGON

## The Deschutes

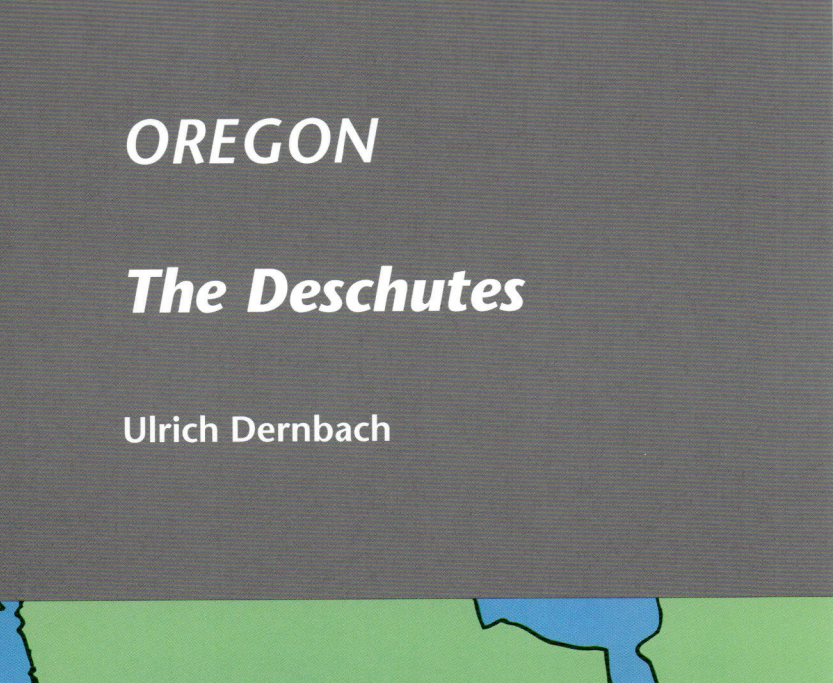

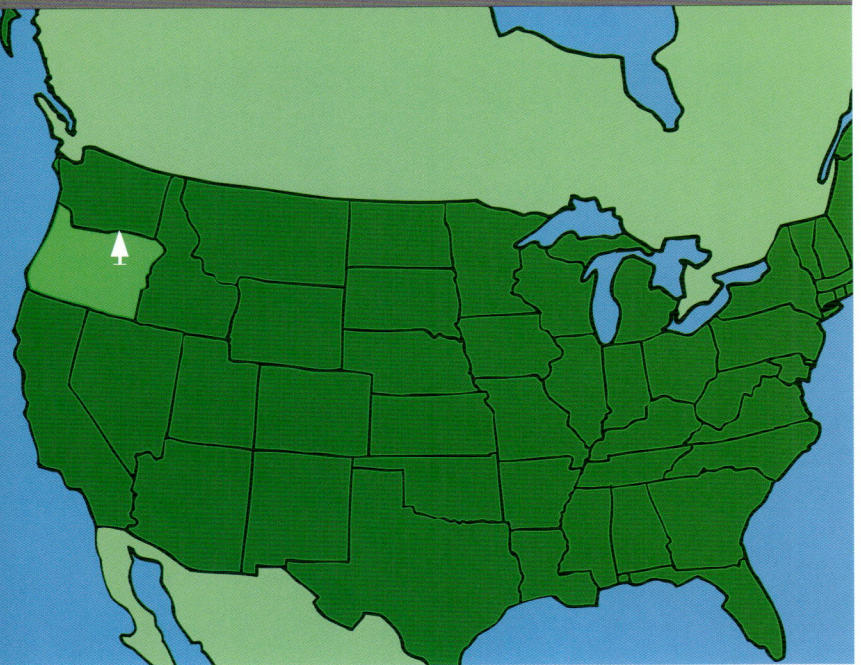

Ulrich Dernbach

**How to Get There**

Drive east along Interstate 84 from Portland toward Salt Lake City for about 100 miles (160 km) along the Columbia River. When you leave the highway at Celio Village you will have reached the Deschutes River (ill. 2.5).

Scattered across an area measuring several hundred square miles, you will find petrified specimens derived almost exclusively from five-million-year-old petrified oak trees (ill. 2.8). These specimens date from the Pliocene, the most recent epoch of the Tertiary period.

Decades ago, many petrified oak trunks could still be found along the Deschutes River, but those days are long gone. The enormous value of these attractive fossils soon become widely known, and that reputation quickly put an end to the beloved pastime of "scavenging" or digging for specimens. Since then, a large portion of the area has become federal property. The Bureau of Land Management (BLM) administrates the sites and determines the amount of petrified wood (by weight) that a private individual is permitted to dig. This limit varies from state to state within the U.S.A., but even at fossil sites located on privately-owned land, you must ask the property's owner for permission before you begin to dig.

**George Gunkel (ill. 2.6)**

When it comes to petrified wood, he's definitely one of the pioneers. The operator of extensive fruit orchards along the Columbia River, it was purely by accident that Gunkel also become owner of the largest collection of petrified oak trunks that I have ever beheld.

It's unbelievable: he actually stacks petrified wood on his land the way other people stack their firewood! (ill. 2.7).

Now 80 years old, Gunkel was one of the first people to recognize the value of these beautiful fossils. His chance of a lifetime came in 1964, when an unusually severe flood inundated the region around the Deschutes River. Floodwaters eroded the riverbank, washing away the soil that had held and hidden hundreds of petrified tree trunks for millennia. No one else seemed interested in the Pliocene "driftwood," so Gunkel had little trouble persuading local farmers to let him collect the petrified wood and store it on his farm.

Ill. 2.5
Deschutes River

Ill. 2.6
left: George Gunkel
right: Dennis Murphy,
two "old pioneers"

Ill. 2.7

Ill. 2.8
Oak with three "hearts"

23

# OREGON

## Stinkingwater

Ulrich Dernbach

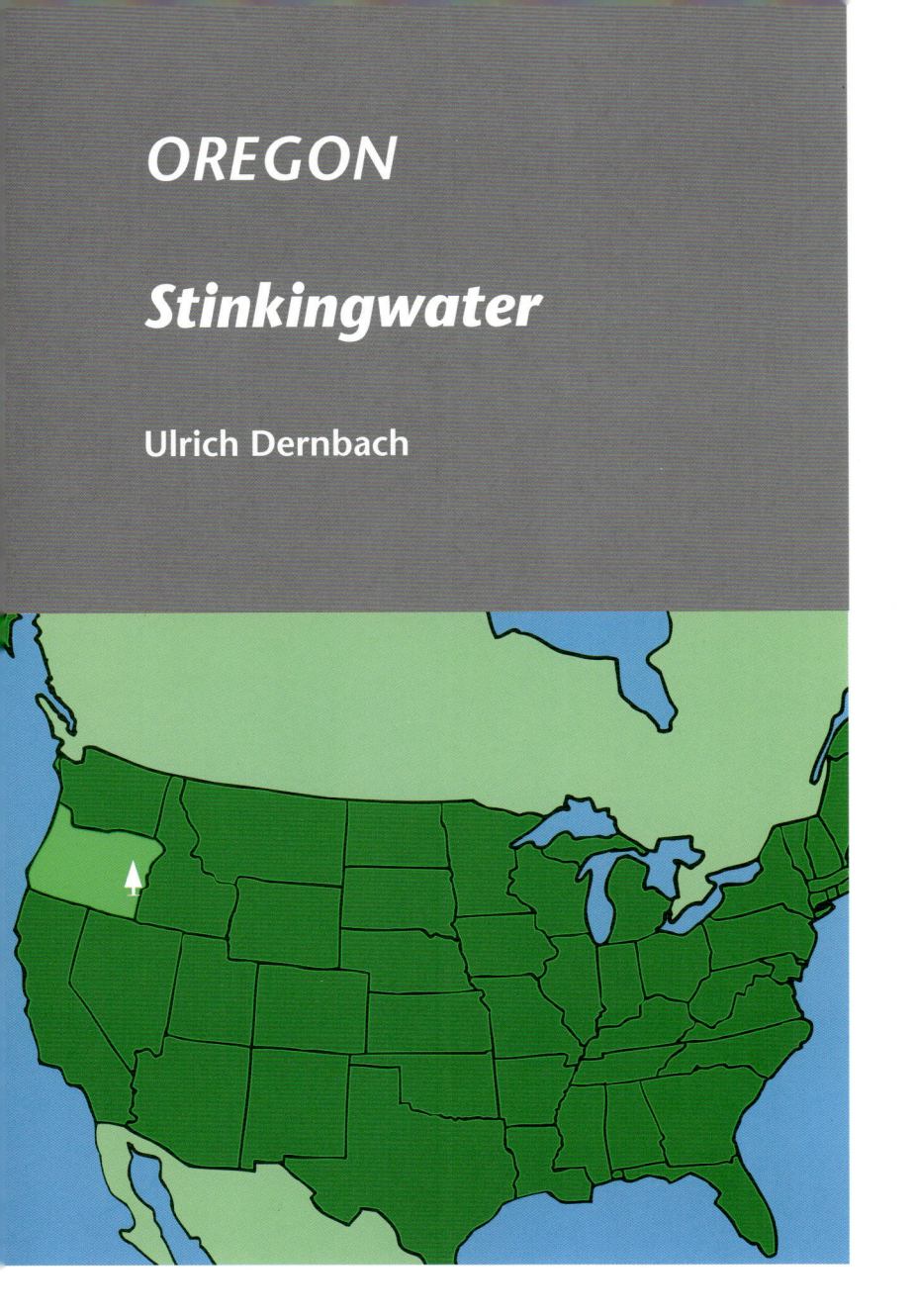

*The name is well chosen. In the summer, when the little brook that folks call "Stinkingwater Creek" shrinks to a rivulet, the neighborhood really does stink of rotten algae.*

You can count yourself lucky if you are fortunate enough to find one of the few Miocene-epoch petrified oak trunks still left here (ill. 2.10). If you hope to find anything at all, come prepared to dig. But if you do find some petrified wood, then by all means do have it cut and polished, because this site has yielded some of the most attractive petrified woods anywhere on Earth (ill. 2.11, 2.12).

As late as 1968, trunks still lay strewn about the area. Since then, the site has come under BLM jurisdiction, so diggers are now obliged to obey the weight limit.

Ill. 2.9
Dan Riegel

Abb. 2.12

### How to Get There

If you're driving from Burns toward Ontario on Oregon State Highway 20, take the first left-hand turn shortly after you cross Stinkingwater Pass. Continue for 5 miles (8 km), then turn right and drive another 2 miles (3.2 km) until you reach the winding valley of sinuous Stinkingwater Creek (ill. 2.9).

Ill. 2.10
From the Murphy family´s treasure trove

Ill. 2.11
"Golden oak"

25

# OREGON

## McDermitt

Ulrich Dernbach

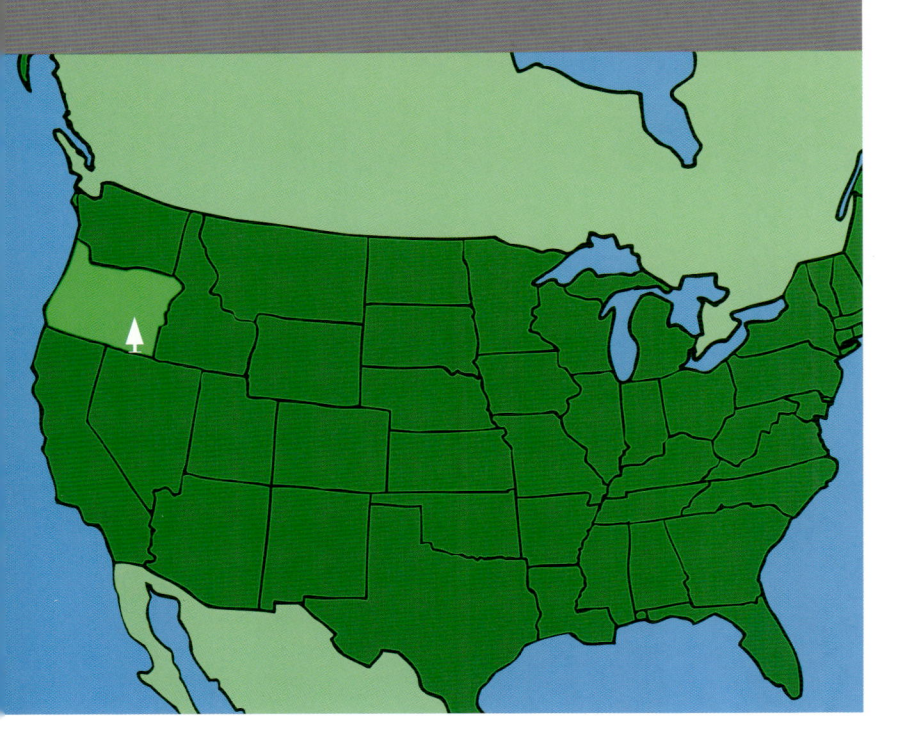

McDermitt Petrified Forest lies along Highway 95, almost exactly on the state line that separates Oregon from Nevada.

Dan Riegel, a successful fossil hunter

### How to Get There

If you're coming from Oregon, turn right just after crossing the intersection in McDermitt, drive past the White Horse Restaurant, turn right into the first small road, then immediately turn left. In about 20 minutes' time you'll reach the

Ill. 2.13

● first site at the abandoned Brett Mine, where cinnabar used to be mined.

You'll see traces of past diggings (ill. 2.13) everywhere you look along both sides of the road. The first collectors didn't arrive here until about 1970; before they arrived, large quantities of petrified boughs and trunks still lay strewn about this site.

Today, however, you'll have to dig at least a few meters to find petrified wood. Most of the petrifications are fossilized relics of Tertiary cherry trees and cherry boughs (ill. 2.14).

● You'll find the second site if you continue along the road, cross Cottonwood Creek, and proceed for another 5 miles (8 km). Come to a halt here and you'll be surprised to find specimens of green petrified wood (ill. 2.15). This unusual coloration is due to the action of algae. Most of the specimens are the remains of Tertiary maple, spruce and/or Norway spruce trees.

● You'll find the third site by continuing another 2 miles (3.2 km) in a northerly direction. There you'll discover a hillside which is practically covered with petrified woods (ill. 2.17). Most of these petrifications are from juniper, spruce and other coniferous trees (ill. 2.16)

Ill. 2.14
Cherry

Ill. 2.16
Silicified cedar

microscopic photograph of cedar,
enlarged 30 times

Ill. 2.15   Wood that has been colored green by algae

Ill. 2.17

27

# UTAH

# The Petrified Forests

Ulrich Dernbach

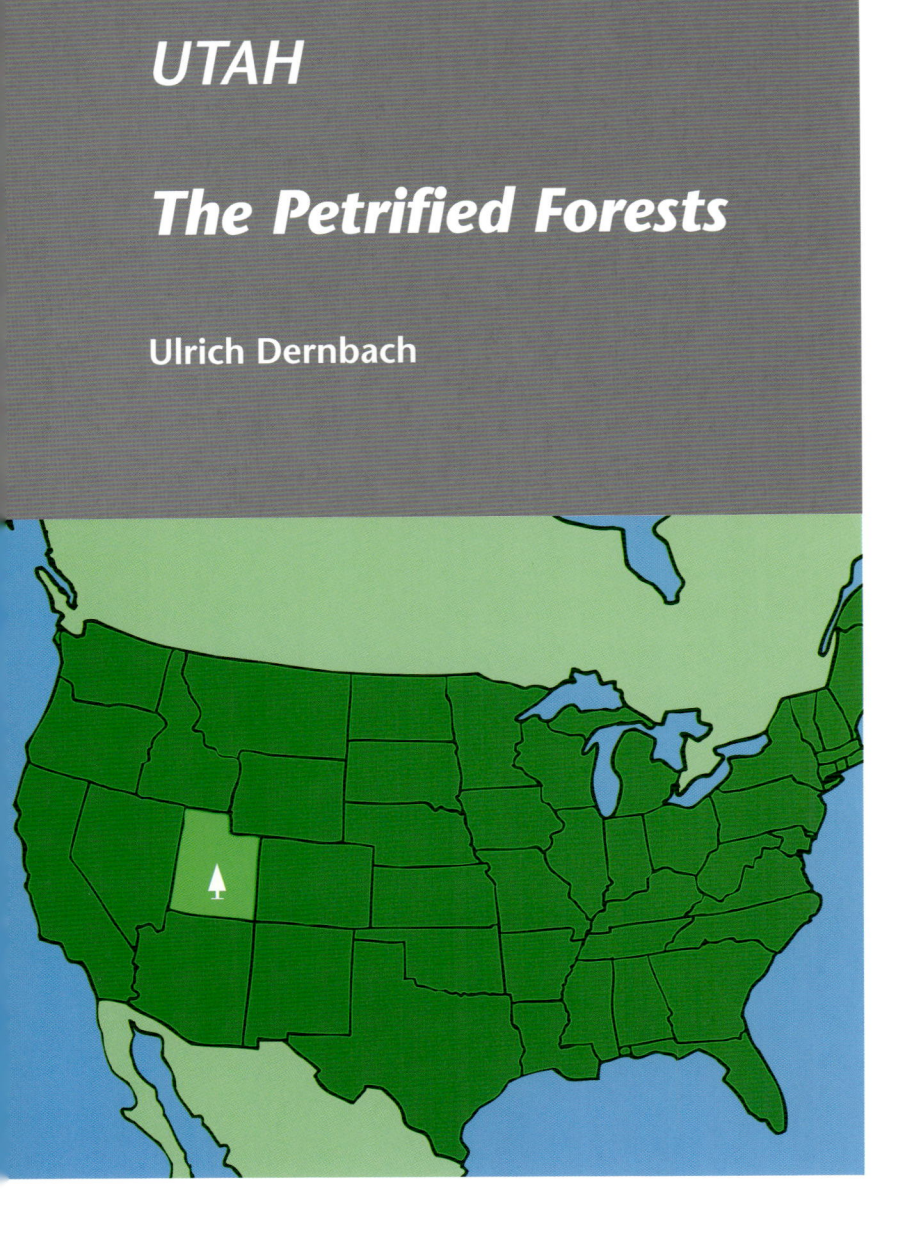

*An imaginary line drawn through the towns of Kanab, Escalante, and Hanksville forms an axis through the heart of Utah's petrified forests. The greatest number of sites are located in the vicinity of Kanab, so I decided to concentrate my search in this region.*

### Splinters and Excavations

Not far from the town of Kanab you can find numerous bits of petrified wood lying on the ground. Many smaller and larger excavations all around suggest that enormous amounts of petrified trunks and branches must have been buried here once, but have long since been removed (ill. 2.18).

This whitish-yellow wood is not especially attractive. Far more spectacular and colorful are the woods to be found at a site about 35 miles (56 km) northeast of Kanab. Because of the poor condition of the road, expect to spend several hours driving from Kanab to your destination. And be prepared to cover the last 3 miles (5 km) either on foot or horseback.

As recently as 1970, people were still finding numerous trunks here, most of them displaying araucarioid woody structure from the Triassic Chinle Formation. Today, this unique site has been thoroughly explored, and you'll have to dig if you hope to find any of the gorgeously colored petrified wood that no doubt still remains hidden here.

It's simply astonishing to see that these petrified trunks have acquired precisely the same coloration as the surrounding landscape: both are predominantly reddish-pink (ill. 2.19, 2.20, 2.21).

### Other Extraordinary Sites in Utah:

South of Hanksville you can search for very colorful Upper Jurassic *Cycadophytes.*

● You can also find specimens of the seldom-seen *Hermanophyton,* likewise dating from the Upper Jurassic period (ill. 2.23).

● Specimens of uniquely colored, Lower Cretaceous "red wood" can be found about 30 miles (48 km) south of Price.

Ill 2.19   Araucaria discovery site

Ill. 2.18

Ill. 2.22
Bill Branson, owner of a
unique collection of cycads

29

Ill. 2.20

Ill. 2.21
Gorgeously colored araucaria

Ill. 2.23
Trunk of a *Hermanophyte*

Ill 2.24
"Red Wood"

31

# WYOMING

## Blue Forest Petrified Forest

Ulrich Dernbach

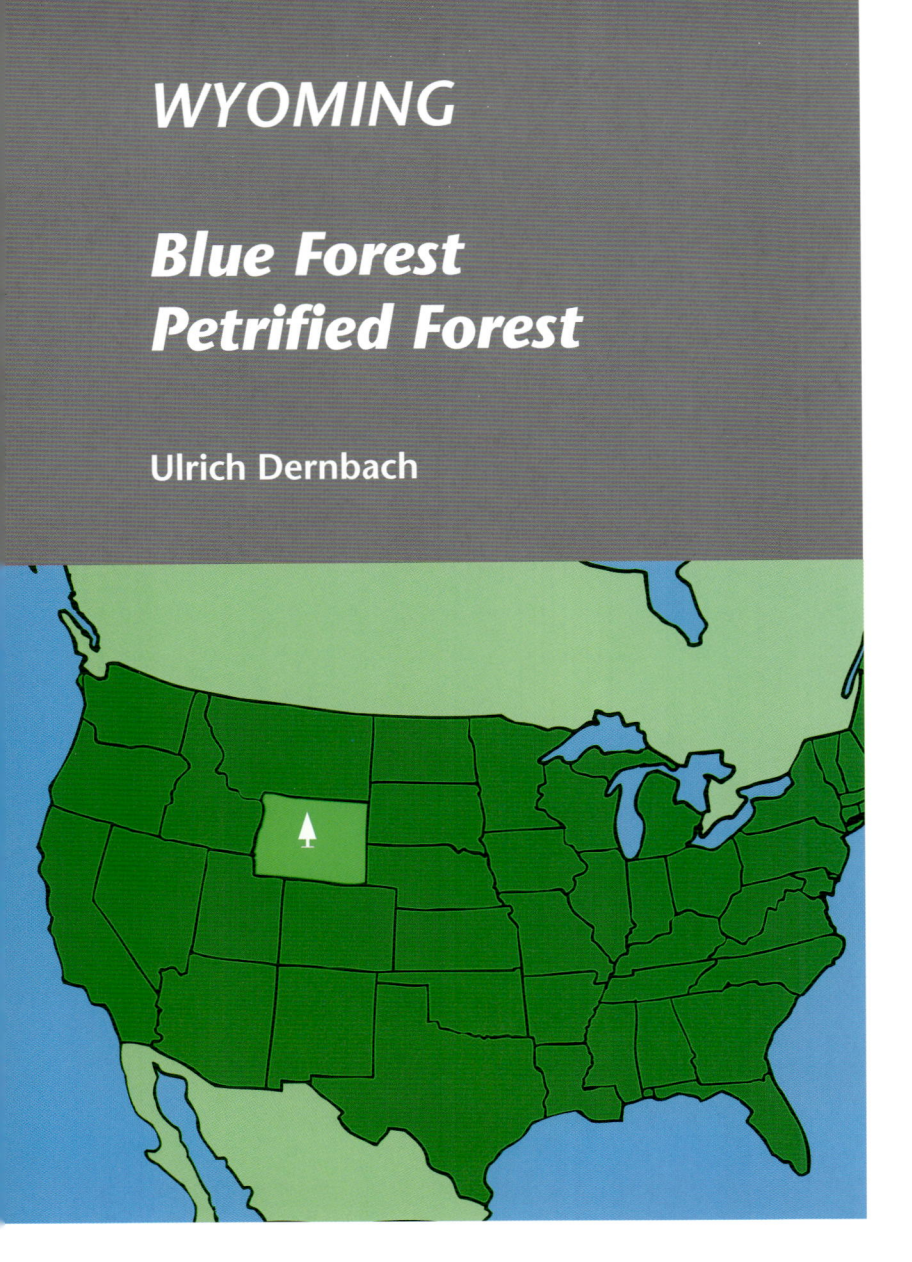

### How to Get There

If you're coming from Kemmerer, drive northeast along Highway 189 for about 20 miles (32 km), then turn right onto Highway 372. Continue for another 11 miles (17.6 km), where you'll reach a stop sign and see the Green River (ill. 2.25). Once across the river, drive straight ahead for another 5 miles (8 km), then turn left. It's not far from here to the Blue Forest.

### The Man with the Divining Rod

Bob Whitmore from Kemmerer knows how to handle a divining rod, but he doesn't use it to search for underground water or veins of gold. He claims to be a specialist at finding petrified wood. And he proved the truth of that claim to me in Blue Forest, Wyoming on September 1, 1995 (ill. 2.26).

### A Forest Below!

Sad but true, one of the world's most beautiful petrified forests lies hidden beneath the earth. The days are gone when one could simply wander through the Blue Forest and stumble upon exciting specimens of petrified wood (ill. 2.27).

Nowadays, all one finds to the right and left of the road are the excavations and other scars left by diggers and fossil hunters. That's why, here too, the magic word is: DIG! But beware: we're on BLM land here and are obliged to observe the collecting limit.

### Blue Forest

The site derives its name from the chalcedony that colored these petrified woods a lovely shade of blue. Many specimens display combinations of chalcedony and quartz. One piece in my collection shows the fully preserved woody structure on one side of the petrified tree trunk and a quartz geode adorning the other side of the specimen (ill. 2.28, 2.29).

This landscape is not only famous because of its petrified wood, but also because the site has yielded an abundant trove of animal fossils. Fossilized fishes, turtles and even crocodiles have all been found here within the so-called Green River Formation.

### The Eocene Epoch -- 58 Million Years Ago

The best-known types of trees from which petrifications have been found include: maple, pine, sycamore, poplar, oak, sequoia and palm (ill. 2.30).

Just 25 miles (40 km) from here is another site where petrified wood can also be discovered: Eden Valley. The woody structure is very well preserved in specimens found at Eden Valley, but these petrified woods lack the striking combination of chalcedony and quartz.

Ill. 2.25  Green River

Ill. 2.26  Bob Whitmore

Ill. 2.27

33

Ill. 2.28
Well-defined woody structure

Ill. 2.29
Quartz geode

Ill. 2.30   Palm

# WYOMING

# The Petrified Forest in Yellowstone National Park

Ulrich Dernbach

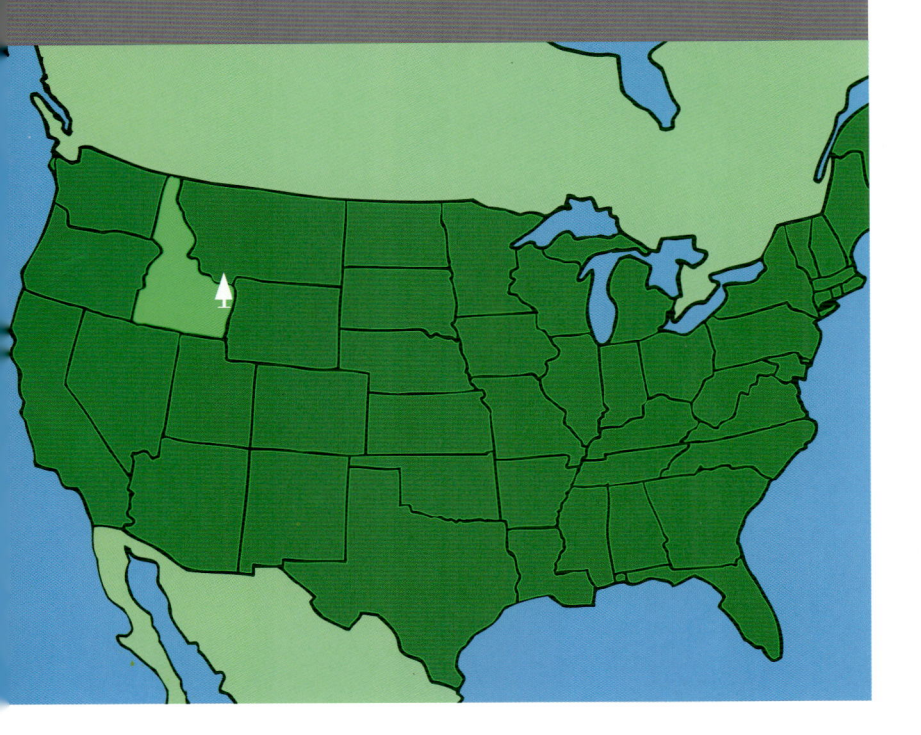

*If someone were to ask which of North America's national parks ranks "number one" in beauty and diversity, the most frequent and entirely deserving winner would probably be Yellowstone National Park.*

The area was declared a national park in 1872. Nowhere are there more geysers (ill. 2.31) and hot springs than here in this region. Likewise impressive are the many species of animals that can be seen in this refuge, where I saw a greater variety of wildlife than I have ever encountered in any other park. Deer and antelope, elk and bison are common, and if you're very lucky you might even see a brown bear or grizzly bear. This park is interesting in so many ways, that you really ought to plan to spend several days here exploring its many remarkable and surprising features.

A tip for sharp-eyed visitors: Don't miss the impressive petrified sequoia trunk to be found not far from Roosevelt Lodge.

**The Petrified Forest**

High up in the mountains, at elevations the hurried tourist seldom visits, you can find one of the most interesting petrified forests that I have ever seen. Standing tree stumps, some of which are several meters tall, are the most exciting feature of this fossil forest. In a few cases, it's even possible to follow the roots of these giant stumps into the soil (ill. 2.32, 2.33). The petrified trees stand at various elevations, with some 1,650 feet (500 m) of altitude separating the lowermost from the uppermost. This situation is probably to be found nowhere else in the entire world. Perhaps the trees were covered by meter-thick layers of volcanic ash during several different epochs.

Scientists have long debated the question: Were the trees in the petrified forest at Yellowstone Park carried here by floods and then petrified or did the forest grow here prior to its being smothered under a thick blanket of volcanic ashes?

William J. Fritz of Georgia University in Alabama lists five major sites where petrifications can be found within Yellowstone National Park. The two best-known sites are Specimen Ridge (ill. 2.34) and Amethyst Mountain Section; lesser-known sites are Mount Norris, Mount Hornaday and Cache Creek.

Ill. 2.31

Ill. 2.32

Ill. 2.34  Specimen Ridge

Ill. 2.35 Ranger Norman Bishop

### How to Get There

If you're coming from Mammoth Hot Springs, drive 18 miles (29 km) toward Roosevelt Tower, then continue 5 miles (8 km) east. Depending on your cardiovascular fitness, it should take you somewhat more or less than an hour to climb the hill. But already halfway up the mountain, your efforts will be rewarded by a chance to see some petrified woods. Don't stop here, though, because the most beautiful petrifications are found at higher elevations.

I was fortunate to have a high-ranking ranger named Norman Bishop along as my personal guide. I'd like to take this opportunity to thank him once again for showing me these extraordinary petrifications (ill. 2.35).

39

Sequoia

### The Eocene Epoch

About 58 million years ago, volcanic eruptions during several different epochs covered old-growth forests with ashes. Sequoia (redwood) was the predominant tree species growing in these forests, but petrifications have also yielded well-preserved specimens of sycamore, walnut, magnolia, chestnut, oak and maple *(Acer sp.)*.

Whether the trees in this petrified forest were borne here by flood waters or actually grew here really doesn't make all that much difference. The fact remains that this is a marvelous and unique site.

Ill. 2.33

# WASHINGTON

## Ginkgo Petrified Forest

Ulrich Dernbach

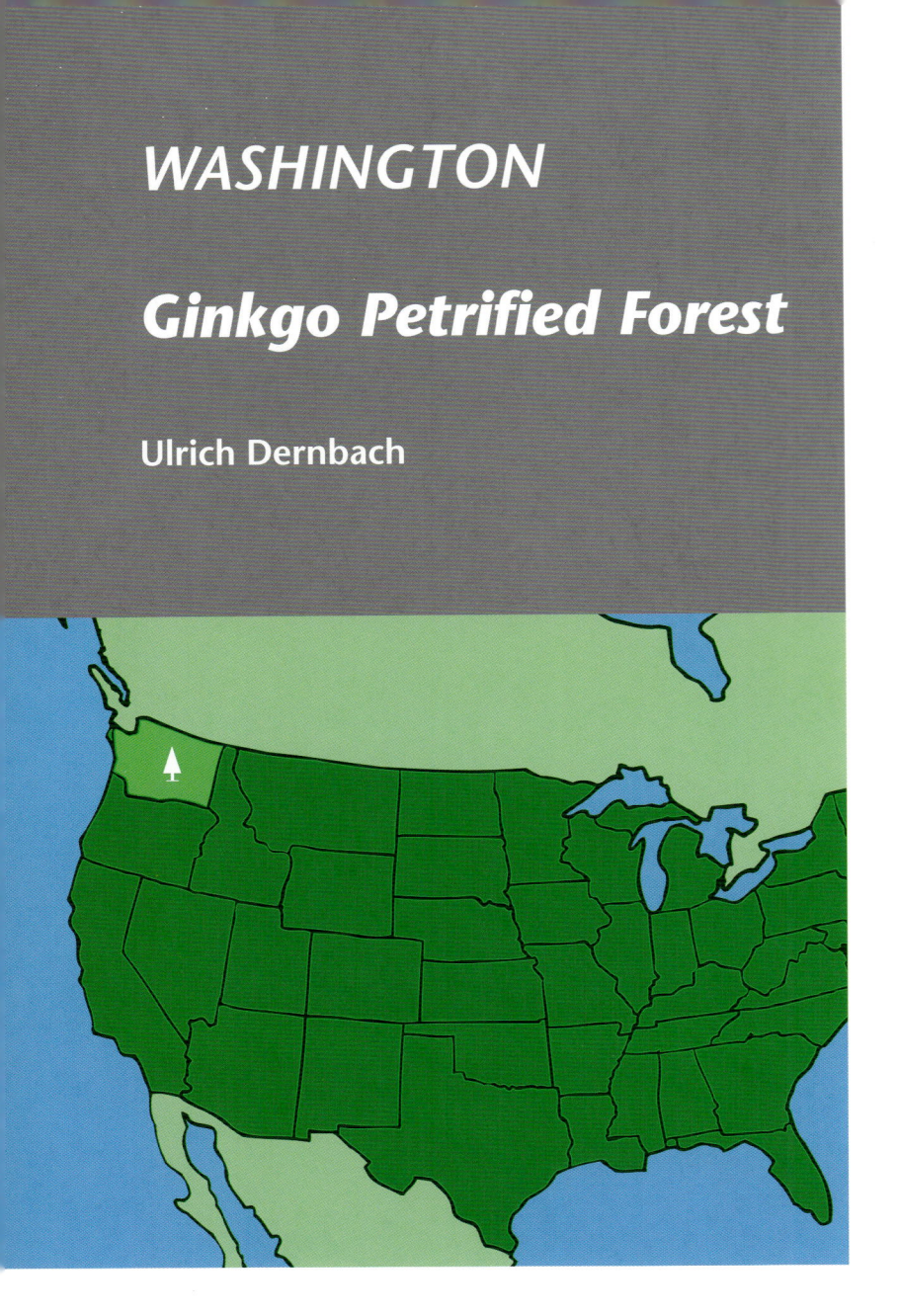

Ill. 2.36

### How to Get There

Vantage is located on Highway 90, about halfway between Seattle and Spokane, in the State of Washington. Taking the Vantage exit off the highway will lead you directly to the petrified forest (ill. 2.36, 2.37). But before you visit the site, be sure to pay a visit to the mineral and fossil shop near the park's entrance. Bill Rose and his family know an extraordinary wealth of information about the forest, and with a little bit of charm you might even be able to persuade him to part with a rare specimen or two from the surrounding area.

### Ginkgo Petrified Forest

This forest and its surroundings have yielded petrified specimens from a greater variety of trees than have been recovered from any other site in the entire world. It is truly a unique place. My informants told me that Professor George Beck of Central Washington College has identified more than 200 different tree species among the this region's petrified woods.

Limitations of space prevent me from listing all of them here, but I will mention a few of the more important varieties: spruce, pine, fir, cedar, maple, oak, elm, magnolia, larch, walnut, birch, alder, beech, sequoia and (of course) ginkgo (ill. 2.38, 2.40, 2.41, 2.42)

*I have known about the petrified woods of Washington State for many years, but not until recently did I manage to acquire some select and very beautiful slices of petrified spruce, elm and maple. These specimens had been found in Vantage, Washington. Not until 1995 did I learn that there is also a petrified forest in Vantage: Ginkgo Petrified Forest.*

Ill. 2.37

And by the way: Ginkgo Forest is the only place in the world where sizeable quantities of petrified ginkgo wood have been discovered.

### Volcanoes

The following sequence of events must have taken place here about 15 million years ago (during the Miocene epoch). Forested highlands were surrounded by countless lakes; torrential rains uprooted trees at higher elevations; floodwaters carried these trees and their broken branches downhill, where they sank into lakes. Later, lava masses from erupting volcanoes poured into the lakes, burying the tree trunks; silicic acid dissolved in the water penetrated the layer of lava, gradually petrifying the submerged wood; various other minerals also dissolved into the solution and were absorbed by the woody tissue, where they bestowed a wide range of colors upon the petrifying wood.

Section of a sequoia trunk

Ill. 2.38 Magnolia

### Attractions in a Heap of Chain-Link Fencing

It should take a little less than an hour for you to walk the loop trail through the the petrified park. In this brief period of time, you'll enjoy the rare opportunity of admiring fossilized trees at 22 different sites.

The only fly in the ointment at this aboveground park is the fact that all silicified trees are secured behind chain-link fencing. That definitely diminishes the aesthetic pleasure of admiring these beautiful relics, but it seems to be a necessary expedient to protect these valuable objects from theft.

Microscopic photograph of magnolia, enlarged 55 times

Ill. 2.39 Ginkgo

Ill. 2.40 *Douglasie*

Ill. 2.41 Spruce

Ill. 2.42 Yew

Microcopic photograph of yew wood, enlarged 27 times

45

# CALIFORNIA

# The Petrified Forest of Calistoga

Ulrich Dernbach

*C*alistoga Petrified Forest simply didn't fit into my itinerary when I visited ten other U.S. petrified forests during the summer of 1995, so I decided to pay it a visit in January 1996.

### Like a Miracle

My plane landed at San Francisco Airport one Saturday afternoon in January 1996 - in the midst of a torrential downpour. Shortly afterwards I found myself sitting behind the wheel of a rented car driving north on U.S. Highway 101. I spent the night in Santa Rosa, not far from the petrified forest. My mood was not what you could call "good," especially when I heard the weather forecaster's prediction of still more rain for the following day. Some friends had told me that this particular petrified forest lies amidst a rather shady mixed deciduous and coniferous forest, which meant that good photos could only be taken on sunny days. On the other hand, my next flight was already booked for Sunday afternoon.

I fell asleep with these gloomy thoughts in my mind. When I awoke the next morning, the first thing I did was walk to the window, and I could hardly believe my eyes: bright sunshine! The clouds had simply blown away. It seemed like a miracle.

### How to Get There

If you're coming from Santa Rosa, drive along route 12 toward Sonoma. About halfway between those two places, turn left into Calistoga Road, which will lead you directly to the petrified forest (ill. 2.43).

### Three or Four Million Years Ago

During the Pliocene epoch, i.e., about three or four million years ago, this area was covered by a lush forest composed mostly of sequoia (redwood) trees. Many of these giant trees were already about 2,000 years old when a volcano erupted on Mount St. Helens just seven miles to the northeast. A cataclysmic storm snapped the huge trees as if they were mere match-sticks. Torrential rains fell, and the fallen tree trunks were covered with mud and lava. Silicic acids (silicates) and various minerals penetrated the fallen giants and saturated one cell after another. The foregoing description is only a supposition, but the theory appears to be substantiated by the fact that the majority of fallen tree trunks are still oriented in the same direction in which they were thrown by the force of the catastrophic eruption.

Ill. 2.43 The entrance to the petrified forest

Fossilized fishes and sea shells found in the petrified forest offer indisputable proof that the region was subsequently flooded by the waters of a sea.

### The Petrified Forest, or, Back to the Present

Of course, I was concerned that despite the sunshine, storm clouds might return at any time, so I made a hurried departure and arrived at the petrified forest early Sunday morning. Too early, it turned out, since the park wasn't scheduled to open for another two hours. Fortunately, there was already a ranger on duty, and he was kind enough to allow me to enter this extraordinarily well-maintained and lovingly appointed park. That admirable condition is no doubt due to the efforts of park manager Linda Lacy, who is also an enthusiastic collector of minerals and fossils herself. It was she who told me that a certain cowherd named Charles Evans first discovered petrified tree trunks here in 1870.

A pleasant loop trail leads the visitor past all major sites. Interpretive signs (ill. 2.44) posted along the path explain all significant details about the petrified forest. And the footweary fossil aficionado needn't worry: this gentle little stroll won't take you more than half an hour (approximately one kilometer = 0.6 mile). You'll walk past ten or twelve different sites where you can marvel at some genuinely impressive trunks as much as 138 feet (42 m) in length with diameters of up to 6.5 feet (2 m) (ill. 2.45, 2.46). The roots of some of these giant sequoias still extend deep into the earth and the standing trunks are impressively illuminated with artificial lighting (ill. 2.47).

I spent several delightful hours in this wonderful national park. Of course, I took no specimens with me when I departed, but I did take along the pleasant feeling of having been privileged to witness a truly remarkable natural monument.

Ill. 2.45

Ill. 2.47

Ill. 2.44

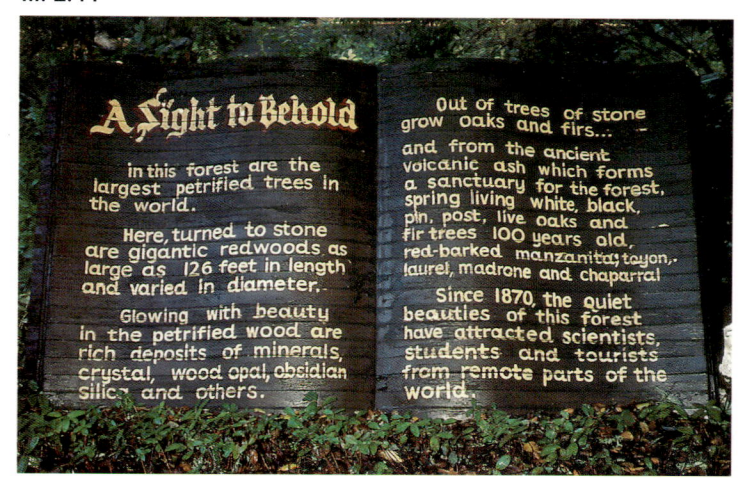

Ill. 2.46

49

# Nevada

# Virgin Valley Petrified Forest

Ulrich Dernbach

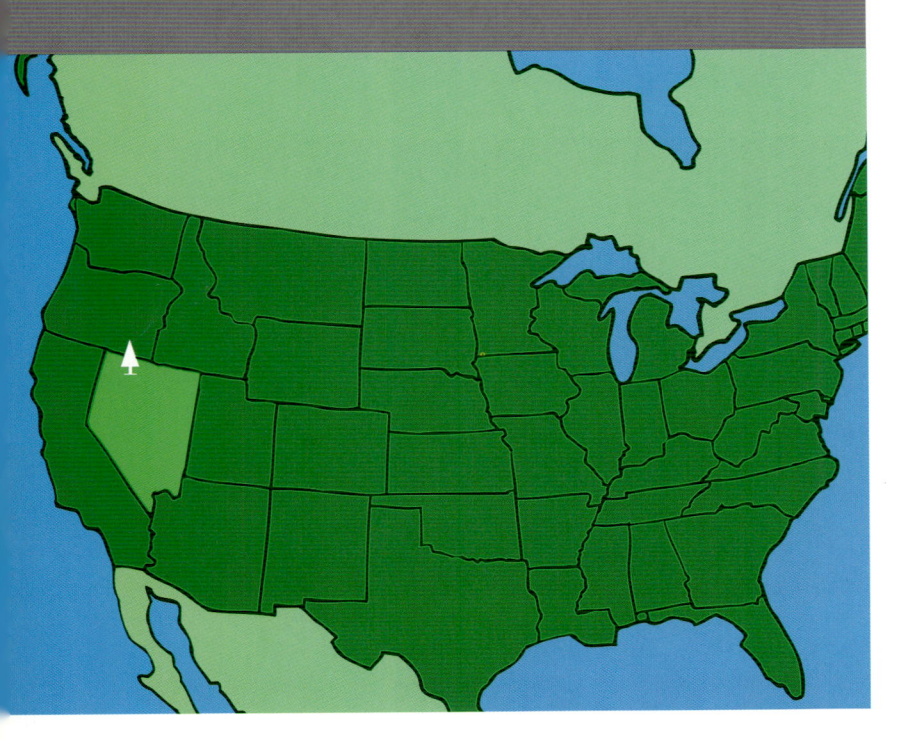

T he opal is without a doubt a fascinating gemstone, but when it occurs in association with petrified wood, then it can make any fossil collector's heart beat a little faster. Of course, I have a few of these rare specimens in my collection.

I acquired most my specimens from Keith Hodson, a man I've known for more than twenty years (ill. 2.48). In the course of those decades, he has frequently repeated his invitation for me to come to Nevada and visit his opal mine. The opportunity finally presented itself in 1994, when I accepted the tempting offer to visit Keith Hodson and his wife Agnes.

**How to Get There**

Virgin Valley Petrified Forest is located in Humboldt County, in the northern part of Nevada. If you're coming from the little town of Denio, then continue driving westward on State Route 140 for about 50 km (32 miles). You'll reach Virgin Valley just a few miles before you cross the Oregon border.

**Virgin Valley**

The landscape around Virgin Valley is not especially attractive. The altitude is over 3,300 feet (1,000 m); you can count the annual rain showers on the fingers of one hand; and nothing but a few scattered sagebrush bushes breaks the monotony of the treeless steppe. You wouldn't think that there would be a lot of animal life in this desolate habitat, but think again: As soon as the evening twilight begins to descend, you can practically feel the high desert come to life. I saw deer and hare several times and once I even caught a glimpse of one of the shy coyotes, but when a herd of wild burros crossed my path, the sensation was really thrilling. The petrified opal forest extends for about 12.5 miles (20 km) across this unique landscape.

**An Accidental Discovery**

If you can believe the tales they tell around here, then it was two cowboys out searching for lost cattle who first stumbled upon the colorfully sparkling opals in 1905. Keith Hodson told me that the next few years brought a veritable "opal rush" to the area. Just like the gold rush in Alaska, opal fever kept the place at a fever pitch for about 20 years. Along with numerous smaller and mostly unrewarding claims, diggings at three particular mines were sometimes quite successful. The situation hasn't changed much today: Rainbow Ridge Mine, Bonanza Mine and the now renamed Royal Peacock Mine still yield the greatest number of gemstones.

A remarkable discovery

Ill. 2.48
My wife Dörte and Keith Hodson

Keith Hodson and his father bought the Rainbow Ridge Mine in the early 1950s. Some years later they acquired the Bonanza Mine as well. Today, however, the family retains ownership of only the Rainbow Ridge claim. Visitors are welcome anytime during the mine's regular business hours: Mondays, Tuesdays, Wednesdays and Fridays from 10 a.m. to 5 p.m. The mine is closed on Thursdays and weekends. For the price of a few dollars' admission, anyone who cares to try his or her luck is welcome to grab a shovel and dig in. The Hodsons sold the Bonanza Mine in 1988. Today, the mine is used by many co-owners who bought their shares for several thousand dollars each. If you want to dig here, be sure to talk with mine manager Bob Kleinschmidt first (ill 2.49).

Ill. 2.49
Bob Kleinschmidt at work

### The Three Layers

Keith Hodson explained that there are basically three layers where opals can be found. The real profits, however, come from stones found in the second and - with a few exceptions - third layer. Keith has found the most valuable, gem-quality, opalized woods in the second layer, which is about 3.3 feet (one meter) thick. In the third layer lies the so-called "conk," a not yet completely silicified wood whose tissue structure is well preserved and which is frequently shot through with layers of very fine opals. These specimens frequently display an especially intensive play of colors and are therefore eagerly sought by collectors.

51

Photo: K. Götz

### Fifteen Million Years Ago

Numerous plants and trees thrived in this region during the Miocene epoch. Identifications of the petrified woods found here have confirmed that spruce, cedar, sequoia, larch, ginkgo, chestnut, birch, elm and oak trees all flourished here fifteen million years ago.

As was the case at other petrified forests, rivers of lava must have overflowed this Miocene forest, killing and burying its trees. Afterwards, silicic acids and minerals filled in the wood cells, gradually transforming the wood to stone. Complex chemical processes which are not yet fully understood led to the formation of the final product: gem-quality opal. Nowhere else except in Australia has this phenomenon been discovered in comparable extent and style.

Section of opalized wood, Photo: G.V. Forster

### Lottery

In the past, many lucky opal-hunters soon found their luck taking a turn for the worse: hairline cracks and tears changed the newly found and apparently valuable specimens into poor-quality wares.

The reason for this deterioration is related to the high percentage of water found within this gemstone. Laboratory analysis has shown that water may comprise as much as 10% of the total weight of some opals. This explains why opals dry out when exposed to high temperatures or strong sunshine. The logical results are tears and cracks.

Many opal hunters protect their valuable specimens by storing them in tanks of water. Others, who refuse to take the warning to heart, simply take their chances - just like playing the lottery.

### The Roebling Opal

The Rainbow Ridge Mine's most beautiful and most valuable black opal was found in 1919. It weighs an impressive 533 grams (2,665 carats).

Despite its age, this stone has lost nothing of its brilliance, and it has not developed even the trace of a tear or hairline crack. According to rumor, Colonel Washington A. Roebling bought the stone for $250,000. He donated his entire collection to the Smithsonian Institute in 1926, where visitors to Washington, D.C. can still admire Roebling's black opal today.

### A Broken Beer Bottle?

Perhaps the most remarkable opal discovery was made by Keith Hodson himself in 1975. He had just succeeded in repairing the hydraulic mechanism on his bulldozer and, after an involuntary hiatus of several days' time, he was finally able to resume work. Keith had just broken a large heap of gravel out of his mountain when he suddenly spotted something glimmering in the midday sun. At first he thought it must be fragments of glass from a broken beer bottle, but he quickly asked himself how a beer bottle could possibly have found its way underground. A few seconds later, he found himself holding in his hands the most beautiful opal that he had ever found. Carefully searching through the rubble, Keith discovered a number of other pieces of opal as well. The total discovery amounted to 8 pounds (3.5 kilograms). In both their play of colors and in their gemstone quality, all of these specimens are of the very highest caliber.

**Beautifully patterned opalized wood**

Gorgeously colored opalized wood

Photo: K. Götz

### Who Has the Prettiest Opals?

Again and again, collectors ask the same question: Where are the most beautiful and most valuable opals found - in Virgin Valley or in Australia?

If one regards the combination of opal with petrified wood as one's decisive criterion, then Virgin Valley surely deserves to be ranked far above Australia.

The so-called "crystal," a pure, clear opal sometimes found in Virgin Valley, is also highly prized for its top quality and lovely play of colors. Aficionados rate those specimens among the finest in the world. Were it not for the risk of impermanence, Nevada's opals would surely deserve to mentioned in the same breath with those found in Australia.

But no matter whether you grant highest honors to Down Under or Way Out West, Virgin Valley Petrified Forest surely deserves to rank among the most significant opal discovery sites in the United States.

### A Fortress

A terrible surprise awaited me when I revisited the Hodsons in the fall of 1995. The area around Rainbow Ridge Mine had been transformed into an armed camp: chain-link fence and barbed wire surrounded the living quarters (ill. 2.50). What had happened?

Several months before, three young men from Los Angeles descended upon the Rainbow Ridge Mine, gunned down Keith Hodson, and stole a sizeable quantity of valuable opalized wood.

Though badly wounded in the shooting, Keith Hodson has since recovered from his ordeal. The three bandits, who were captured soon after the robbery, have all been sentenced to lengthy prison terms.

Ill. 2.50

# ARIZONA

# The Petrified Forest of Arizona

Ulrich Dernbach

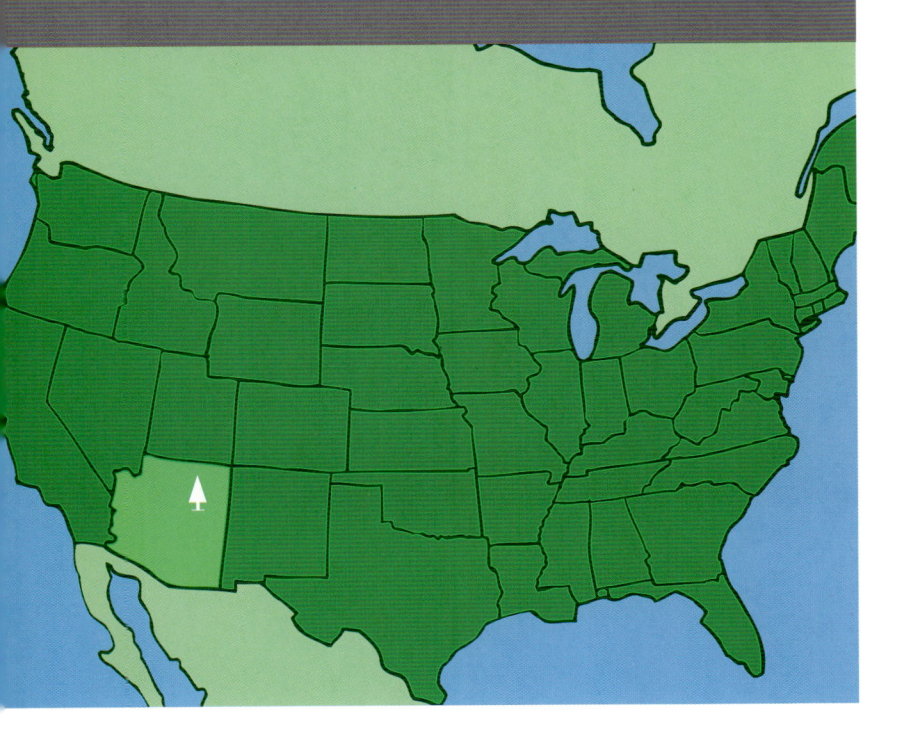

*At least once in his or her life, everyone who collects or appreciates petrified wood should visit the petrified forest in Arizona. It is a truly superlative national park.*

**How to Get There**
Two routes lead to the petrified forest.

● If you drive west along Interstate 40 and get off at exit 311, you'll soon arrive at the park's northern gate.

● Or if you're coming from the west and are planning to continue eastward after visiting the forest, you're best advised to get off the interstate at the Holbrook exit, then follow Route 180 toward St. Johns. You'll reach the park's southern gate after traveling for about 19 miles (30 km).

**Petrified Forest National Park**
Since I have always spent the night in Holbrook whenever I visited the site, the park's southern entrance has always been more convenient for me.

After walking only a few steps into the park, you'll soon meet a ranger who will give you a brochure containing all necessary information. And you'll be expressly reminded that you will be penalized if you attempt to remove fossil wood or other historical objects.

Despite the close watch kept on visitors, rangers estimate that about two tons of petrified wood are stolen every year. That's all the more incomprehensible, since inexpensive and very attractive specimens of petrified wood are readily available for purchase both inside and outside the park's boundaries.

Leave your car at the visitors' center, then walk a short way uphill from the building to see the "Long Logs." A little path leads you from there to the "Giant Logs," some of which measure as much as 99 feet (30 m) in length and 4 feet (1.2 m) in diameter (ill. 2.51).

Inside the visitors' center you can learn more about the history of this petrified forest.

Between 6000 B.C. and 1450 A.D., the region was inhabited by native people. Relics of their culture which can still be admired today as silent witnesses to this prehistoric civilization include Puerco Pueblo, Newspaper Rock and Agate House - a dwelling built entirely of petrified wood.

When a railroad line was built across the region in 1880, many people discovered the petrified forest for the first time. Gemstone hunters shattered dozens of trunks hoping to find valuable minerals hidden within the petrified trees. At some

Ill. 2.51

discovery sites, mills were erected to manufacture industrial abrasives from the silicified wood. Irreplaceable natural treasures were destroyed forever during those early years.

On December 8, 1906, U.S. President Theodore Roosevelt established the Petrified Forest of Arizona as America's second national monument, but the site was not declared a national park until December 9, 1962.

Equipped with this interesting information, you are now ready to begin your adventure-filled drive through the Rainbow Forest and the Painted Desert. Parking is available at all points of particular interest. Foot paths lead from the parking facilities to individual attractions.

Bright colors and striking crystal structures are found in many silicified trunks in Jasper Forest and Crystal Forest.

Blue Mesa features several exciting discovery sites. Here you can witness erosion gradually uncovering petrified trees. After many years of erosion, the

Ill. 2.52 Agate Bridge

petrified specimens eventually break free of the soil and tumble down the steep slope.

Agate Bridge (ill. 2.52) is also definitely worth seeing. An especially long petrified trunk bridges a small canyon here. According to legend, a cowboy named Paine agreed to ride his horse across the narrow natural bridge, and earned ten dollars for his (and his horse's) steady nerves!

Also worthy of note is the uneven distribution of giant trees within the park. In some places they are so abundant that they actually lie one atop the other; elsewhere you can walk for miles without sighting a single petrification, although researchers believe that these seemingly empty sites actually hold petrified materials at depths of about 330 feet (100 m).

An alert observer will no doubt notice that nearly all of the rootless, horizontal trunks are oriented in the same direction. This uniformity, together with the fact that only a very few petrified boughs or twigs have been found here, lend support to a theory which claims that all the petrifications found in this national park were carried here as driftwood by tremendous floods which swept them

**Eroded over millions of years**

from an ancient forest that once grew some 94 miles (150 km) from the park's present location.

### 225 Million Years Ago

During the Triassic period, in the Chinle Formation, this region enjoyed a tropical climate. The northern part of Arizona was a huge, low-lying plain whose elevation seldom exceeded more than a few meters above sea level. During this period, Arizona lay rather close to the Earth's equator - about 1,700 miles (2,720 km) closer than its present location. Swamps and rivers meandered across the landscape; lush vegetation provided food and habitat for numerous prehistoric animals.

Thus far, fossil relics of 60 species of fauna and some 200 species of plants have been found within the park. Various fishes and shellfish lived in the rivers, crocodile-like phytosaurs, armored reptiles and giant amphibians (metoposaurs) ruled the habitat. Extensive plains supported rich forests of ferns, cycads and arboreal horsetails. Enormous coniferous forests thrived at somewhat higher elevations. Araucarias of the species known as *Araucarioxylon*

All illustrations on this page: *Araucarioxylon arizonicum*

Ill. 2.53

60

Enlarged 48 times

Ill. 2.54 *Schilderia adamanica*

*arizonicum* (ill. 2.53) were quite common; *Schilderia adamanica* and *Woodworthia arizonica* (ill. 2.55) were also present, but in lesser numbers.

If you are so inclined, you can spend hours roaming through the petrified forest here in Arizona. If you want to see every attraction and walk along every path and loop trail, you should plan to stay a second day.

June, July and August are the months when the park receives the most visitors. These three months account for nearly half of the annual guests, which is quite a large crowd when one considers that no fewer than 923,000 people visited the site in 1994!

The park's summertime popularity is no doubt due to the scheduling of vacations and to the pleasantly warm temperatures of these months, when daytime highs

Ill. 2.55 *Woodworthia*

regularly range from 90° to 100° F (32° to 38° C). But beware: temperatures plummet during the late afternoon and early evening because the Rainbow Forest lies at an altitude of some 5,900 feet (1,800 m).

After you reach the prehistoric Puerco Pueblo ruins and cross the Santa Fe railroad track, you'll enter the so-called Painted Desert. Here again it will be worth your while to drive to several different scenic overviews. The visibility is excellent here, and the palette of colors among the scattered volcanic cones and flat-topped mesas is simply magnificent. Depending on the weather and the angle of incident sunlight, the landscape can present a wide spectrum of gorgeous colors ranging from pale pink to dark red and deepest indigo.

After so much natural and cultural stimulation for the eyes and mind - most people need at least five hours to explore their way from the park's southern to its northern entrance - your stomach might well be calling for some stimulation too. Now's the time for a perfectly grilled steak like the excellent ones you'll find waiting for you at the steakhouse in nearby Holbrook.

Forty-year-old postcards

Ralph Thompson, a world-renowned petrified-wood merchant, posing in front of a spectacular longitudinal section

# ARGENTINA

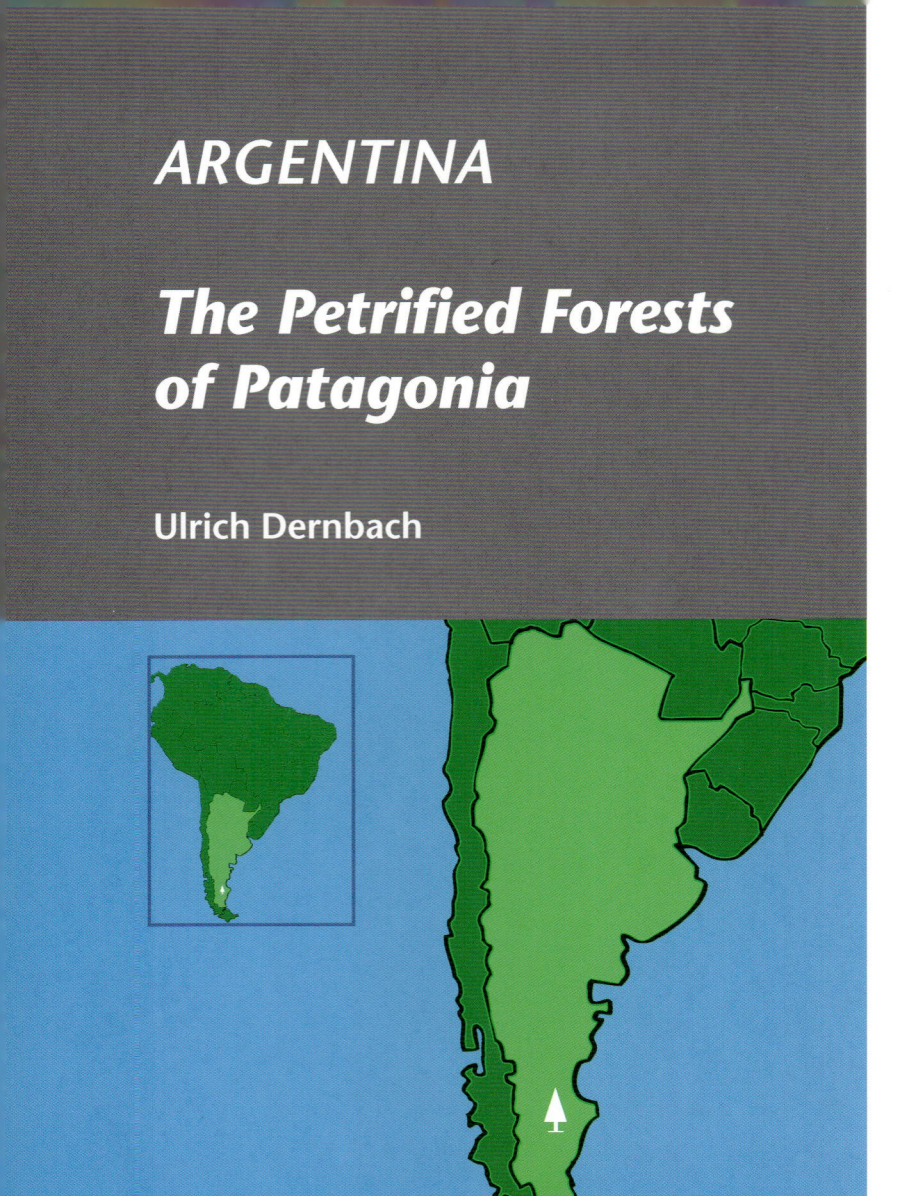

## The Petrified Forests of Patagonia

Ulrich Dernbach

Ill. 2.56

W hen I wrote the book *Araucaria* back in 1992, I did not yet know that three impressive petrified forests could be found in Patagonia.

Ill. 2.57

Ill. 2.58

Ill. 2.60

Ill. 2.61 Araucaria with worm-eaten tunnels

## *Cerro Cuadrado Petrified Forest*

### How to Get There

Leave Comodoro Rivadavia and follow National Route 3 toward Rio Gallegos. Drive through the little town of Fitz Roy, continue another 56 miles (90 km), then turn left into a small road. Follow that road for another 25 miles (40 km) and you'll arrive at the petrified forest.

### From the Tertiary to the Triassic

For many years, experts disagreed about the age of the petrified forest known variously as "Cerro Cuadrado" or "Jaramillo." Some scientists claimed that the forest flourished during the Triassic, others insisted that it was of Tertiary provenance, until learned opinion finally reached a consensus: this is a Jurassic-period forest.

Ill. 2.62

Ill. 2.64

66

### Giant Trees, 115 Feet (35 M) Tall

When you first set foot in Cerro Cuadrado Petrified Forest, you'll notice a sign reminding you that collecting petrified wood or other fossils is strictly prohibited. You are strongly urged to obey these rules, not only because park wardens enforce them to the letter.

Depending on your mood and degree of enthusiasm, one or two hours' time should satisfy your curiosity about this primordial forest. Extremely lengthy silicified tree trunks can be found here: lengths of 115 feet (35 m) are by no means seldom, and many trunks boast diameters up to 5 feet (1.5 m) (ill. 2.56, 2.57, 2.58).

These giant trees reminded me of the "Long Logs" in the petrified forest in Arizona. Cerro Cuadrado Petrified Forest has earned special fame thanks to the excellently preserved conifer cones (*Araucaria mirabilis* [ill. 2.59] and *Pararaucaria patagonica*) that can be found here. These cones only reveal their full beauty when they are cut in half and polished. Like the petrified woods, the cones also display a gorgeous array of red, yellow and blue colors. Though many millions of years old, some of these cones still display excellently preserved petrified seed kernels (ill. 2.64).

The most commonly found trunks thus far identified at this site belonged to araucarioid trees (ill. 2.60, 2.61, 2.62). Relics of a few scattered cycads have also been discovered (ill 2.63).

Ill. 2.59

Ill. 2.63
*Cycadeoidea* - a rare discovery

# ARGENTINA

## José Ormaechea Petrified Forest

Ulrich Dernbach

I first visited Cerro Cuadrado Petrified Forest in 1987. Not until 1993 did a confidential tip inform me of the existence of little-known José Ormaechea Petrified Forest.

### How to Get There

The journey begins in Comodoro Rivadavia. This time, though, you stay within Chubut Province and drive directly toward Sarmiento. A narrow little road diverges to the left at the edge of town, and a prominent sign announces that you are on your way toward the petrified forest, which you should be able to reach after about another hour of driving.

### Dinosaurs

But before you leave Sarmiento, be sure to pay a visit to the local museum with its lovingly arranged displays. Present-day natives of Sarmiento proudly describe their home town as "The Capital City of the Dinosaurs," so it's little wonder that these gigantic former citizens are the museum's paramount attraction.

### The Petrified Forest

I've looked at a great many maps, but I've never found one that includes mention of this beautiful petrified forest. Since the forest seems to have eluded cartographers, it has remained relatively unknown. Nor have I found it mentioned in any of specialized literature about this subject. If one can believe the little brochure on sale at the gate, then this forest was petrified during the Tertiary period, i.e., about 65 million years ago. To date, no one knows which species of trees were silicified here.

You'll need at least two hours if you want to see everything, but your patience and perseverance will be richly rewarded. You'll find gorgeous tree trunks up to 99 feet (30 m) in length with diameters up to 6.6 feet (2 m), but the terrain around them is rather uneven so be sure to wear sturdy shoes (ill. 2.65). Some trunks are quite well preserved, and traces of roots (ill. 2.66) can be seen on a few individual specimens. The most fascinating sites are where you can find petrified trunks extending directly out of the mountainside (ill. 2.67).

Only a few scattered bushes are able to survive in this desert landscape. One almost feels as if one were walking on the surface of the moon, rather than across the barren hills of Argentina on the planet Earth.

Ill. 2.65  A massive trunk, 99 feet (30 m) long and 6.6 feet (2.0 m) thick.

Ill. 2.66

Ill. 2.67

Araucarias

# ARGENTINA

## Szlapelis Petrified Forest

Ulrich Dernbach

*This petrified forest is completely unknown. You're not likely meet any tourists here; at most, you might happen upon a wandering gaucho.*

### How to Get There

Since this "forest" is only two hours away from José Ormaechea Petrified Forest, you really ought to pay it a visit. You'll be glad you did.

Follow Route 26 toward the little town of Rio Mayo until you see a sign along the road directing you toward Szlapelis Petrified Forest. After about 30 minutes of driving, the road had deteriorated so much that we were obliged to continue rolling along at walking tempo.

Which really wasn't so bad after all, since we suddenly found ourselves at the edge of a steep ravine: the entrance to Szlapelis Petrified Forest (ill. 2.68).

### Fitness is Essential

Sturdy boots and good physical condition are a must for anyone planning to begin carefully picking his or her way down the steep hillside. After a few meters' descent you'll spot the first giant silicified trees lying at the foot of the hill (ill. 2.69, 2.70). Since Szlapelis Petrified Forest is part of the same formation as nearby José Ormaechea Petrified Forest, we once again find ourselves in the midst of a Tertiary-period forest.

However, the area covered by Szalpelis Petrified Forest is considerably smaller than that occupied by its neighbor.

I took me a little less than an hour to see everything. Afterwards I began the strenuous ascent. Making it back to the car definitely puts some demands on one's physical fitness - or one's lack thereof!

Ill. 2.69

Ill. 2.70

Ill. 2.68

Lovely markings on a small araucarioid trunk

73

# BRAZIL

## The Petrified Forest at Sao Pedro do Sul

Ulrich Dernbach

### How to Get There

Petrified wood can be found along the entire length of BR 287 from Santa Maria (Rio Grande do Sul) all the way to the little town of Mata. The petrified forest itself, however, lies about halfway between those two cities, on the city limits of Sao Pedro do Sul.

### Museum

We arrived in January 1994 and were cordially welcomed by biologist Sylvia Salla, who generously offered to show us around the petrified forest.

Of course, first we took a thorough look at Sao Pedro do Sul's museum, of which Sylvia Salla is the director. All major discoveries of the past few decades are lovingly displayed here. Several dinosaurs caught my eye, but what really attracted my attention were the petrified woods. As I had expected, they were exclusively coniferous woods from the Triassic period.

*Can you believe that somewhere in the world there is a small town whose buildings are built largely from blocks of petrified wood? It's amazing, but nonetheless true: there is indeed such a place. It's called Mata and is located in the extreme southern part of Brazil in Rio Grande do Sul Province, not far from Sao Pedro do Sul Petrified Forest.*

Ill. 2.71
Araucarias

Thousands of tree trunks have since been collected and purloined by natives and by gemstone hunters, although the trade and export of petrified wood has been illegal in Brazil for quite some time. Sylvia suspects that if roads were better in the region around Sao Pedro do Sul, then everything of value here would surely have been carried off too. Fortunately, there are still plenty of petrified trunks, perhaps derived from trees related to the araucarias. It is still possible to find gorgeous petrified trunks, some as much as 66 feet (20 m) in length, embedded in the deep green foliage of this lush natural landscape. Some pieces are nearly 39 inches (one meter) in diameter (ill. 2.71, 2.72).

Ill. 2.72

### The Petrified Forest

Sylvia Salla had made excellent preparations for our expedition, as evidenced by the fact that a VW bus and driver were already waiting for us when we left the museum.

Later, I would be very glad that we accepted these amenities, since the landscape surrounding the petrified forest is very hilly and the roads are in extremely poor repair. Sylvia explained that it used to be possible to find petrified wood all along the 50-mile-long (80-kilometer-long) stretch of road between Santa Maria and Mata.

Ill. 2.73

Brazil´s beautifully figured araucarias

This is one of the rare sites where a visitor can compare fossil araucarias with numerous living araucarias *(Araucaria angustifolia)* that still flourish here (ill. 2.73).

### Almost Unbelievable

The little town of Mata lies just half an hour from Sao Pedro do Sul. When I first set foot in this village, I was confronted with a very special surprise. Everywhere I turned, my gaze fell upon petrified wood!

Entire piazzas and streets are paved with petrified wood, staircases and several-meter-tall walls are built entirely of petrified tree trunks. It's absolutely sensational (ill 2.74, 2.75).

No doubt the sight of so many valuable petrifications used for such mundane purposes will turn the stomachs of palaeobotanists and collectors, but this unique town is nevertheless a must-see for tourists and for anyone else interested in petrified wood.

Ill. 2.74

Ill. 2.75

Sylvia Salla and Brazilian friend Decio Freitas

# BRAZIL

# Araguaina Petrified Forest

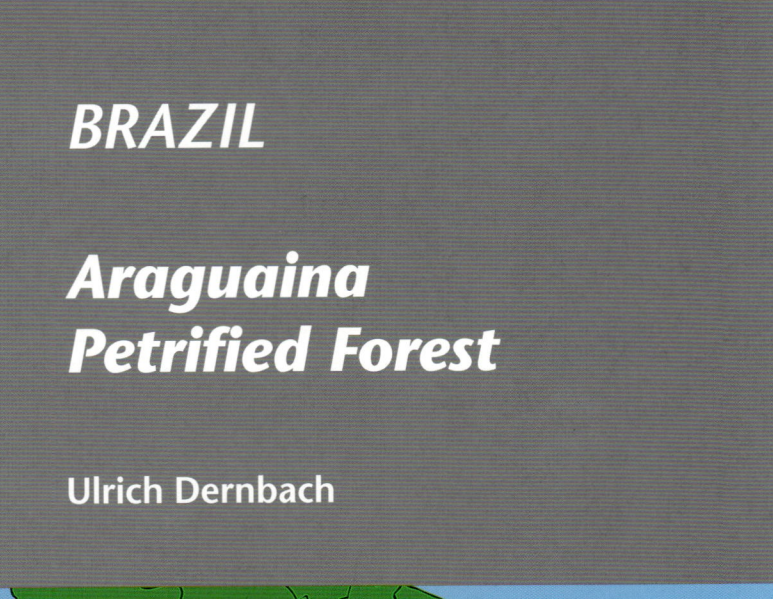

Ulrich Dernbach

*Except for the local native people, few human beings have ever seen the petrified fern forest at Araguaina. If I hadn't visited this forest, the book you are now reading would have been one attraction poorer.*

### How to Get There
From Araguaina (in Maranhao Province), take the road toward Babaculandia (39 miles/62 km). Immediately before reaching the little city, turn left into the petrified forest.

### 280 Million Years Ago
During the Lower Permian period, i.e., about 250 to 280 million years ago, a wide range of plant and tree species must have flourished in this region. Thus far, however, only the tree fern *Tietea singularis*, some types of horsetails, and some specimens of araucarioid wood have been positively identified.

### An Adventurous Flight
I scheduled my visit to the petrified forest at Araguaina for June 1994. Since the month of June occurs during the southern hemisphere's winter season, I had reason to hope that my expedition would be blessed with bearable temperatures. Unfortunately, those hopes would prove unfounded, as you'll find out later in this report.

The flight began smoothly. I boarded the plane in Sao Paulo together with my wife and my Brazilian friend Decio Freitas, and a few minutes later we were airborne. Our itinerary called for us to change planes in Brasília, then fly another five hours to Araguaina, our final destination (ill. 2.76).

Everything went well until we landed in Brasília, where it was announced that our connecting flight would be delayed for 3 1/2 hours. No explanation nor any

Ill. 2.76 Araguaina Airport

reason for the delay was forthcoming. When we were finally able to board our plane, we were told that in order to make up for the delay, the flight would not land at Araguaina at all, but would continue directly to Sao Luis on the Atlantic Coast instead. Since travelers in South America soon learn not to worry about clock time, we took the news calmly. Although our sojourn in Sao Luis cost us another four hours' delay, we were treated to a free 1,250-mile (2,000-kilometer) flight and an evening meal on the airplane.

## A Strenuous Endeavor

We woke early the next morning, hoping to make an early start in order to avoid the midday heat. And indeed, by nine o'clock that morning we had already reached the fork and turned into the road which would lead us directly toward the petrified forest. My suspicions were aroused by the fact that this road seemed to be getting narrower and narrower, and those suspicions soon became dreadful certainty when we came around a bend and saw what remained of the road abruptly disappearing into the savannah.

A grueling, several-hours-long hike lay ahead of us. The mercury had already climbed to 86° F (30° C), and temperatures were still rising. But worse than the heat was the humidity, which must have been nearly 100%. Despite these strenuous conditions, the hike was an unbelievably beautiful experience. The landscape was very attractive and diverse. We crossed valleys, climbed over small hills, passed gorgeous palms and beguilingly fragrant blossoms where colorful parrots nibbled on tropical fruits (ill. 2.77, 2.78). Were it not for the stifling heat, we might well have believed that we had wandered into the midst of paradise.

More than three hours had already gone by when we reached a small grove of trees. Beyond them I saw a few small huts. Renaldo, our guide, explained that we were now very close to the petrified fern forest.

One cannot simply march right into the ancient forest, because all of the petrified woods lie on private property. Permission is absolutely essential. I have always found the natives to be quite friendly, but if you trespass on their property, they can sometimes be very unpleasant - and they always carry weapons.

Ill. 2.79

Ill 2.80

## Ferns, Ferns, and More Ferns

We were very fortunate: not only did we receive permission to enter the petrified forest, but a young native boy agreed to lead us to the largest and most beautiful fern trunks. I counted as many as 200 petrified trunks along a stretch of just 330 feet (100 m). Some trunks, though broken, attained the respectable lengths of 40 feet (12 m) and diameters of about 24 inches (60 cm) (ill. 2.79, 2.80).

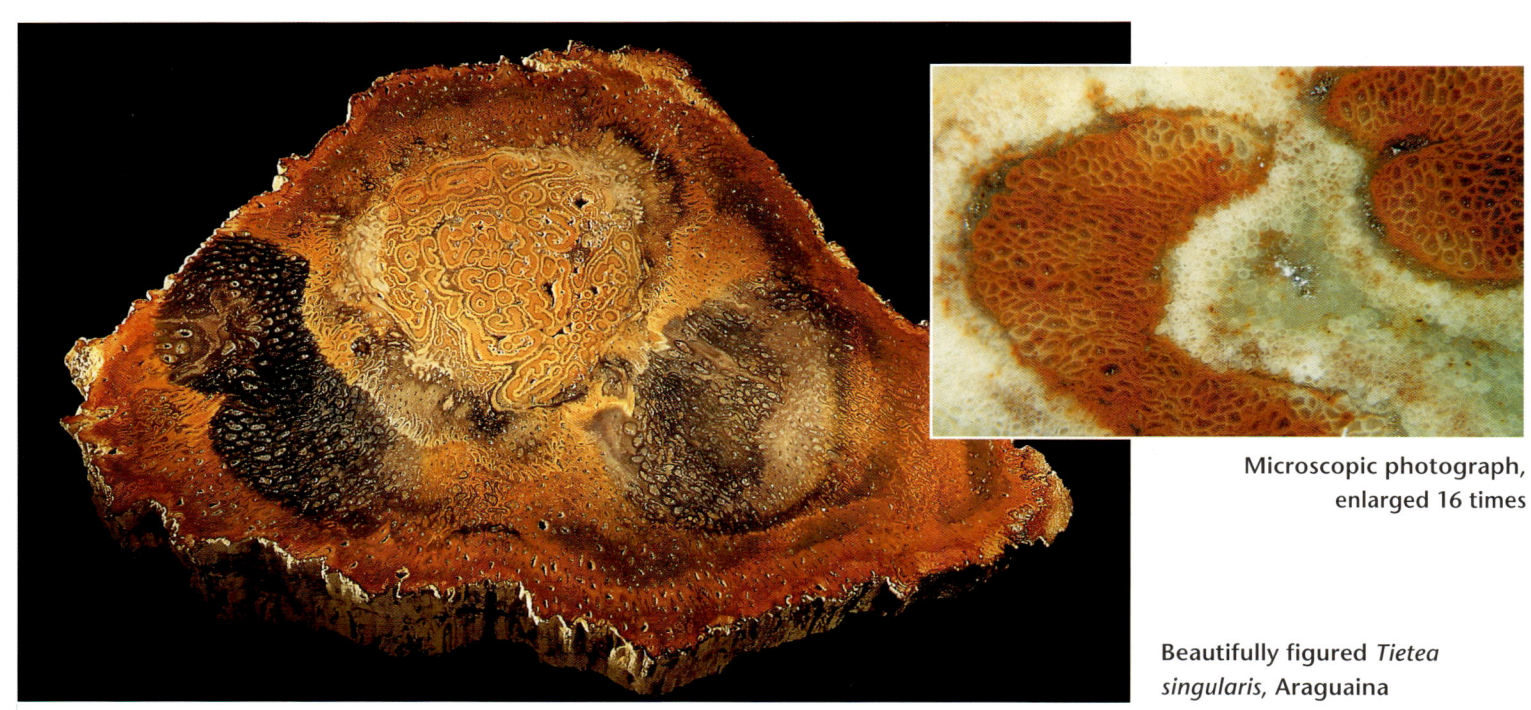

Microscopic photograph, enlarged 16 times

**Beautifully figured *Tietea singularis*, Araguaina**

## You Just Have to Be Lucky

I had already taken quite a few photos when I noticed a fern trunk with unusually lovely patterning. I decided to photograph it in an upright position for variety's sake, so I stood it on end, took the picture, and let it fall a few seconds later.

It was then that I saw that I had grasped the trunk in the narrow space between two scorpions - live scorpions, of course. Sometimes you just have to be lucky.

Araucarioid wood, Araguaina

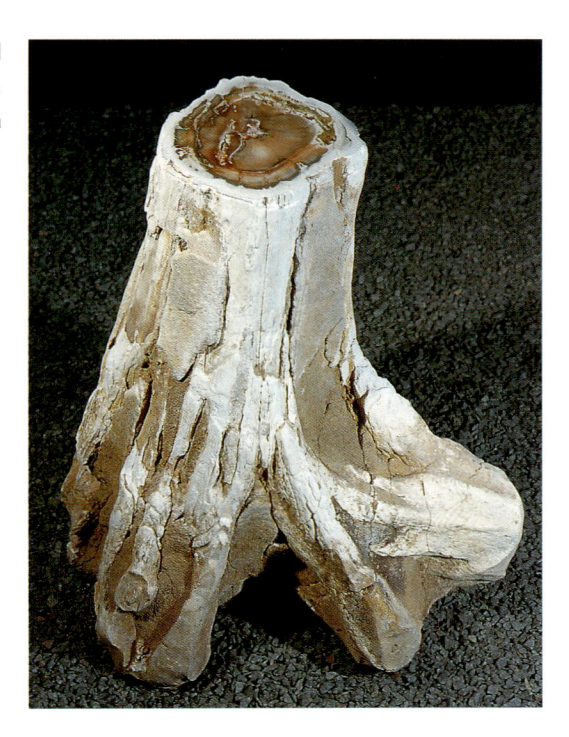

## A Special Discovery

Permian forests were not monocultures exclusively composed of tree ferns. Although we encountered a great many petrified tree ferns here, I also expected to find specimens of *Medullosa*, araucarioid woods and horsetails. I kept my eyes peeled, but wherever I looked, all I saw were tree ferns. Suddenly my wife called out. She had stumbled upon a lengthy, petrified trunk which did not look at all similar to the many tree fern trunks that we had seen thus far. Although the specimen was quite dirty, I was immediately certain that she had discovered a tree-sized horsetail fossil. I was absolutely overjoyed when our native guide presented me with this horsetail and another small fern trunk as gifts.

After we had refreshed ourselves with a few juicy oranges, we bid farewell to our guide, leaving him with a generous tip that made it difficult to say which of us was more delighted with the day's events. And I'm sure that we'll always be greeted as welcome guests if and when we ever visit this remarkable site again.

Horsetail, Araguaina

Microscopic photographs, enlarged 28 times

# EGYPT

# The Petrified Forest of Cairo

Ulrich Dernbach

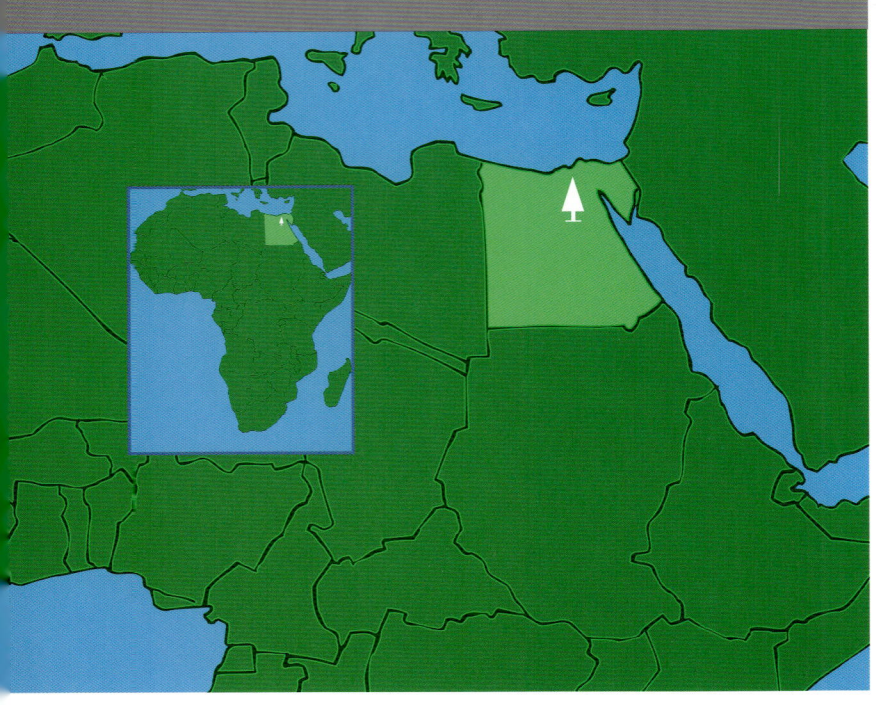

Ill. 2.81

Naturally, most foreigners who visit Cairo are attracted to its numerous mosques and palaces and especially to its pyramids (ill. 2.81). But even the city's regular inhabitants are not likely to know that a remarkable petrified forest can be found near the city's limits.

**How to Get There**
From the Al Maadi neighborhood, travel down the main road toward Suez, which will lead you past numerous quarries, industrial parks and refuse-disposal sites. After 10 miles (16 km) you'll reach a row of toll booths. Six-tenths of a mile (1 kilometer) further on you'll find the petrified forest, where a large sign "Petrified Forest" alerts you to turn left off the main road.

Ill. 2.82

I first visited Cairo in 1986, and even then that city with its 14 million inhabitants seemed rather chaotic. I paid my second visit to the city in May of 1996. During the intervening decade, Cairo's population had increased to 17 million, not including the outlying suburbs. Wherever one looks, one sees new construction going up, as the city continues its unrelenting expansion into the desert.

Ill. 2.84

### The Petrified Forest

Cairo's petrified forest was placed under state protection as a natural park in 1989. Park geologist Ahmed Salama Mohamed explained to me that it was not officially opened to the public until in 1996.

Petrified tree trunks measuring up to 99 feet (30 m) in length with diameters in excess of 39 inches (1 meter) are scattered across an area of some 3.8 square miles (0.6 square km) (ill. 2.82, 2.83).

The geologist said that this petrified forest is about 35 million years old (Oligocene). Scientists believe that the tree trunks were deposited here by floodwaters millions of years ago, where they were subsequently silicified under masses of lava. Support for this hypothesis is provided by the fact that traces of roots, smaller silicified branches, fruits and leaves have never been found here. The precise identity of the trees preserved here has not yet been determined.

Ahmed Salama Mohamed noted that research is currently underway to identify the species of trees petrified here. Thin sections of the petrified woods are expected to yield reliable results in the near future. Existing literature reports that Stenzel, Schweinfurth, Kräusel, Stromer and others all found the petrified remains of conifers, palms and deciduous trees in the greater Cairo area (ill. 2.84, 2.85).

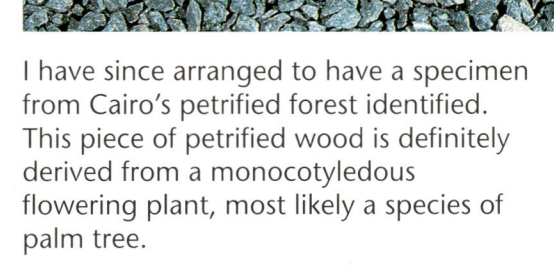

I have since arranged to have a specimen from Cairo's petrified forest identified. This piece of petrified wood is definitely derived from a monocotyledous flowering plant, most likely a species of palm tree.

Ill. 2.85

Ill. 2.83

# NAMIBIA

## The Petrified Forest of Namibia

Eike Pätz

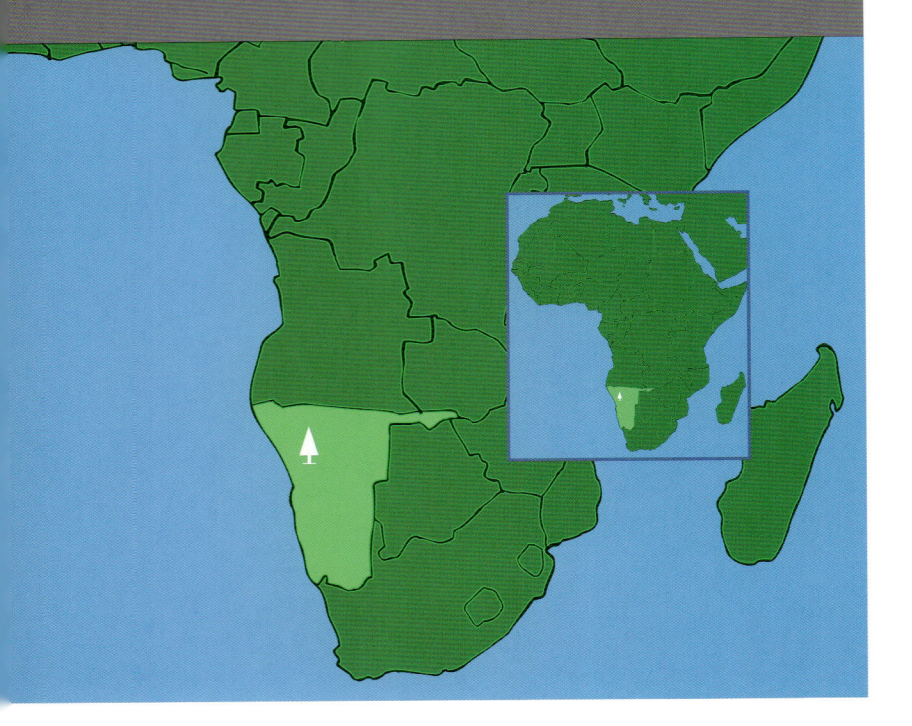

Namibia is a mineral-rich country in southwestern Africa. The nation is especially well known for its not inconsiderable reserves of diamond, tourmaline, topaz and beryl.

Although one doesn't generally associate Namibia with petrified forests, an impressive example of this type of natural wonder can be found in the northwestern province of Damaraland. Here one can pay a rewarding visit to what is known in the Namibian language as the "Versteende Woud."

**How to Get There**

The ideal point of departure for a visit to the petrified forest is the place called Khorixas. Along with 40 bungalows, Khorixas also offers camping facilities, a swimming pool, and (especially worth mentioning) an excellent restaurant. A 26-mile (42-kilometer) journey along an unpaved track bearing the number 39 leads you directly from Khorixas to the petrified forest.

Ill. 2.86  Photo: E. Pätz

**The Petrified Forest**

You'll know you've arrived when you see a large sign announcing (in three different languages) that you have entered a petrified forest and that the collection or removal of petrified wood is strictly forbidden.

The site was declared a national monument back in the early 1950s, but it stood unguarded until 1993.

It's advisable to explore the gently rolling landscape on foot. Depending on your degree of enthusiasm, one or two hours' time should suffice. Millions of years after their petrification, trunks measuring up to 99 feet (30 m) in length have now been exposed by erosion. With circumferences of approximately 19.7 feet (6 m), most of these massive trunks lie parallel to one another (ill. 2.86).

This uniformity, together with the fact that no smaller boughs, roots or cones have been found here, suggests that the

The petrified forest of Namibia. Photo: E. Pätz

Ill. 2.87 Triassic needle-bearing tree, Namibia. Collection: Fremder

Ill. 2.88 Collection: Fremder

trees were deposited here by floodwaters. It is almost certain that the trees did not grow at this site, but were uprooted elsewhere and swept down to this site by cataclysmic floods. Although diurnal temperature changes can be excessive in Namibia, and despite the continual erosion at work here, these petrified woods are still in a remarkably good state of preservation. Even delicate features such as knot holes and traces of annual rings are readily seen. Most of these silicifications range from pale to dark brown in color; reddish shades are rather uncommon (ill. 2.87, 2.88).

### 200-Million-Year-Old Araucarias?

Palaeobotanists believe that these petrified woods are the remains of needle-bearing, araucarioid trees. The age of the petrifications is estimated at about 200 million years.

85

# ZIMBABWE

# The Petrified Forest of Zimbabwe

Rüdiger Hesse and Ben Macray

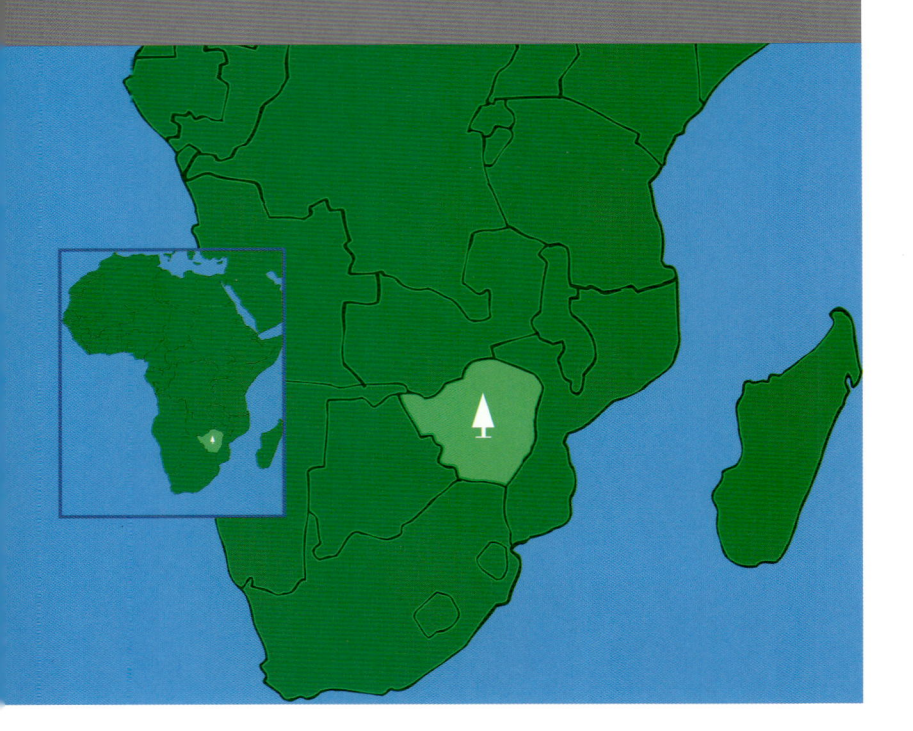

The first time I vacationed in Zimbabwe, one of the sites I visited was the market in Harare, the capital city of this African nation. Of all the wares on sale there, what interested me most was the petrified wood, lovingly displayed as slices, small boughs or book-ends.

The branches, whose diameters ranged from 1 to 20 inches (3 to 50 cm), were marvelously well preserved; even the bark was still visible on some specimens. Certain pieces showed traces where branches had been attached, and, when cut and polished, some of these woods revealed an intensive green color (ill. 2.89).

Ill. 2.90

Of course, I was eager to learn where I could find such attractive specimens, since, after all, I am a collector, and what could a collector love more than searching for and finding his own fossils?

The next day I was most fortunate to meet Ben Macray. A Frenchman by birth, Ben had lived in Zimbabwe for the past several years. He offered to escort me to the petrified forest.

**How To Get There**

We drove west from Harare for about 93 miles (150 km) until we reached the little town of Kwe-Kwe. From here, the journey continued directly into the discovery site called Gokwe. The road out of Kwe-Kwe deteriorated drastically, and most of the time we found ourselves driving along loosely packed, sand-covered tracks. We were glad that we had rented a jeep equipped with four-wheel drive. The landscape was varied and for the most part heavily forested. Ben explained that we were passing through Majunga-busi National Forest.

Leaving the forest behind, we drove past many large plantations where cotton, corn (maize) and tabacco were being cultivated.

Ill. 2.89

Ill. 2.92

### The Petrified Forest

Our vehicular journey reached its end about 19 miles (30 km) west of Gokwe, but we still had 7.5 miles (12 km) to cover on foot. Hiking mostly downhill, we crossed terraced mountainsides, descended 396 feet (120 m) in altitude, and finally reached the petrified forest some three hours later. Petrified branches and trunks were strewn all over the area. Ben explained that the greater portion of the petrified forest still lay buried beneath the surface, and added that fossilized wood had been discovered all over an 18.6-mile-wide (30-kilometer-wide) area (ill. 2.90, 2.91).

Although our visit took place during the winter, the temperature was an uncomfortably warm 86° F (30° C), so we decided to collect only a few specimens of petrified tree trunks to carry back in our rucksacks. But I was determined to return soon, and I vowed to bring along some local men to help me transport my discoveries. I was absolutely enchanted by the petrified wood of Zimbabwe.

Ill. 2.91

Ill. 2.93

**Triassic Araucarias and *Woodworthia***

The petrified forest of Zimbabwe is largely composed of araucarioid wood (ill. 2.92). Very attractive specimens of *Woodworthia* are less common, but sometimes found nonetheless (ill. 2.93). This petrified forest is belived to be about 200 million years old (Triassic).

# MADAGASCAR

## The Petrified Forest of Madagascar

Ulrich Dernbach

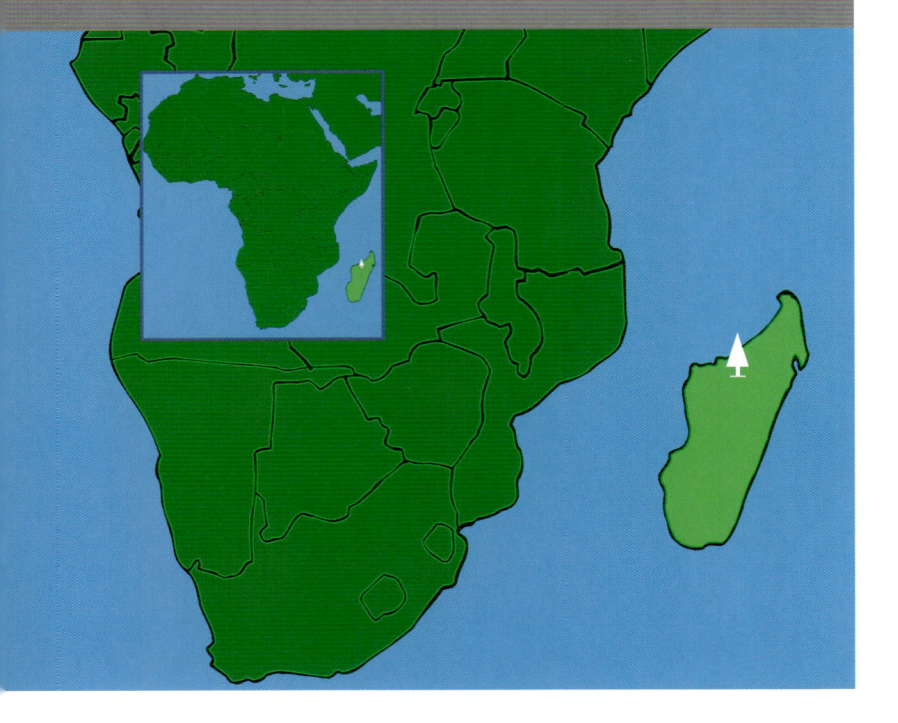

I had been looking forward to visiting Madagascar for a long time, not only because no book about fossil woods would be complete without a description of the petrified forest found on this large island in the western Indian Ocean. As you'll learn by reading the following account, my long-awaited expedition to this petrified forest would ultimately prove to be a rather sobering experience.

### Description of the Discovery Site

Petrified tree trunks can be found throughout the entire western region of the island from Mahajanga to Toliara, but the most abundant collection of silicified woods is found east of Maintirano.

Other impressive sites lie in the Morandava Depression and scattered across the terrain on both sides of the road that links Skahora with Toliara.

I decided to focus my search on the site east of Mahajanga.

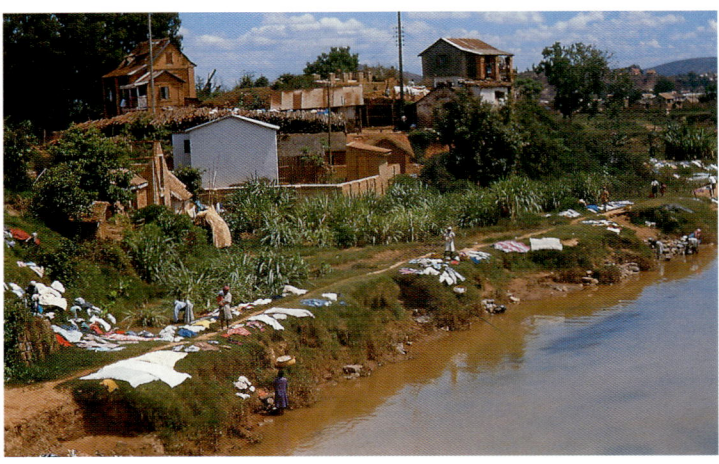

"Laundry and communications center" for the women of Antananarivo

### Antananarivo

My Madagascan adventure began on December 14, 1995 when I boarded a plane at Frankfurt Airport. After thirteen hours' flight time and a stopover in Nairobi, we were glad to arrive safe and sound in Antananarivo, the capital city of Madagascar. Although only 12.5 miles (20 km) separated our hotel from the airport, it took our taxi three hours to get there. The narrow streets of the capital city are hopelessly overcrowded, and it is not uncommon for the slowly moving traffic to stop completely for long periods of time.

The next day I had ample time to arrange for the rental of a sturdy vehicle suitable for the expedition we had in mind. I rented a compact, four-wheel-drive jeep from an Indian fellow. I was pleasantly surprised to learn that the rental price also included the services of a driver. We arranged to depart the following morning.

I was glad to leave the crowded capital, where the pushing and shoving of too many people in too little space was not at all to my taste. It seemed as if everywhere I turned, impoverished young mothers with infants or small children were stretching their empty hands toward me. Some of these people were downright aggressive. We also had to remain constantly vigilant against pickpockets. You can imagine my relief when our expedition got under way six o'clock the next morning. But shortly before we departed, I was compelled to make an important decision: our driver asked me to let him to take his wife along with us; my two travel companions were less than enthusiastic about the idea, but I decided to grant our driver's request, since I knew how much more pleasant it would be to spend our five-day expedition with a good-humored driver rather than with a surly chauffeur. Later on, as it turned out, I would have no cause to regret my generosity, since the driver's wife proved to be a constant source of optimism and a veritable fountainhead of good vibrations.

### Mahajanga

Leaving Antananarivo behind us, we drove along Route 4 toward the coastal city of Mahajanga, which, according to our map, lay some 375 miles (600 km) to the northeast. Everything went along smoothly at first. The road was passable and we made rapid progress. We were crossing a high plain where an altitude of about 3,300 feet (1,000 m) created pleasantly bearable temperatures.

Ill. 2.95
Another unexpected obstacle

About 62.5 miles (100 km) further on, we descended from the plateau, whereupon the temperature rose abruptly and the condition of the road become absolutely catastrophic. Deep potholes forced us to drive at a snail's pace. Although it was not yet midday, the mercury had risen well above 86° F (30° C). We were obliged to interrupt our journey with frequent pauses. Whenever we passed through little villages, we stopped to refresh ourselves at so-called "hotels" (ill. 2.94), but we dared drink nothing except bottled Coca-Cola. "Hygiene" seemed virtually unknown in this country. Thousands of flies crawled over the dishes served to us, and it was not uncommon to find dead animals lying directly in front of the restaurants. Our driver and his wife seemed completely unperturbed by the unappetizing surroundings: I've never seen two people enjoy their meals with more thankfulness, deeper humility or greater pleasure than this couple displayed at table with us.

Throughout our trip, I had been wondering why there were no telephone wires on the telephone poles along the roads. I asked our driver, and he soon put an end to the mystery. It seems that when Madagascar became independent of France back in the 1950s, the local people cut down the telegraph wires, which the French had painstakingly strung, and used the strong, pliable cables to tie down the straw on the roofs of their huts. This also explains why only a few cities in Madagascar can be reached by telephone.

Ill. 2.94
A so-called "hotel" on Route 4

### Like the Middle Ages

Eleven hours and 250 miles (400 km) later we suddenly found ourselves at the wrong end of a gigantic traffic jam. What seemed like an endless parade of motionless trucks stood bumper-to-bumper for kilometer after kilometer. Fortunately, the road was just barely wide enough for us to pass them. Of course, all of us were curious to discover the cause of this enormous traffic jam.

Ill. 2.96
Our faithful jeep made it through this trial too

Three days earlier, we now learned, the little bridge near Tsanamandrosa had collapsed under the weight of an overloaded truck. And that was that (ill. 2.95). The fallen bridge severed the only connection to Mahajanga. When - or if - a bridge on Madagascar would ever be repaired was a question whose answer was known only by the gods, and they weren't likely to be holding a press conference any time soon. It might take a week, or maybe a month, who knows? I'd felt as if suddenly been transported back to the middle ages.

Fortunately, our rented vehicle was equipped with four-wheel drive. Some local teenagers showed us a route, we and our vehicle waded into the rapidly flowing stream, and I didn't dare to hope that we would actually succeed in fording the river without getting stuck halfway. Fifteen anxious minutes later we reached the other shore, scrambled up the bank with all our wheels spinning, and left the ruined bridge behind us (Ill. 2.96).

We hoped to reach Mahajanga in about three hours. And indeed we did, just in time to avoid getting drenched by a violent thunderstorm that descended upon the city a few minutes after we did. The rain continued until early morning, reminding us that we had come during the rainy season.

### A Fine Piece of Work

We arranged for our driver to meet us at six o'clock the next morning. Eager to begin the final leg of our journey to the petrified forest, six a.m. found us impatiently awaiting departure. All our gear was carefully packed and everything was ready for the journey, except for two small details: no driver and no car.

An hour later we were relieved to catch sight of the vehicle creeping toward us. When our car and driver finally reached the hotel, we understood why they were making such slow progress: the driver and the rented jeep were finally here, but the windshield wasn't. Our faithful chauffeur excitedly explained that during the night unidentified thieves had removed the windshield in order to steal the radio. Fortunately, instead of breaking the glass, they had carefully cut away the rubber molding that held it in place, then gently

Ill. 2.97

Ill. 2.98 The petrified forest of Mahajanga

Ill. 2.99

A Madagassy-style tomb: the coffins rest atop a pile of petrified wood

removed it and set it aside without damaging the glass. It really was a fine piece of work.

### A Malaria Attack

Since the windshield itself was still completely intact, our resourceful chauffeur got to work installing it. By ten o'clock that morning he had skillfully reinserted the glass and fixed it in place with a hand-sewn leather band. We were finally ready to continue our petrified forest adventure.

We resumed our journey by driving back to Route 4, intending to turn into Route 6 near Ambondromamy, then drive the final 15.6 miles (25 km) into the region surrounding the petrified forest. But the best laid plans of mice and men often go astray... as they did today.

We finally succeeded in putting the 31.2 miles (50 km) behind us, when our driver began to complain of a splitting headache. His ordinarily healthy brown complexion was pale as ash and beads of sweat appeared on his brow: our chauffeur was suffering an attack of malaria.

Ill. 2.100
Our cabin in the jungle

Ill. 2.101

After a brief stop for a strategy meeting, we decided to turn the car around, drive back to Mahajanga, and spend the rest of the searingly hot but culinarily fascinating day in town. It was here that I ate the best - and least expensive - lobster of my entire life.

### The Big Disappointment

The next morning began without a hitch. It took us just three hours to reach Route 6, the road that would lead us to our long-awaited destination. Although a mere 15.6 miles (25 km) separated us from the petrified forest, we were obliged to proceed at walking pace. The clayey soil of the unpaved road was treacherously soft and covered by what seemed to be a shallow but miles-long puddle which made it nearly impossible to avoid driving into enormous potholes that seemed eager to swallow us and our vehicle. We crept tenaciously onward, passing many trucks and cars that had gotten themselves and their passengers hopelessly stuck in the soggy morass. Despite the nearly impassable road, in two hours' time we managed to reach the little settlement where we had agreed to meet our guides. And indeed, there they were, patiently waiting for us to arrive. Two tall, powerfully built Madagassies invited us into their hut and announced that although the petrified forest was only 6.3 miles (10 km) away, it was simply impossible to reach it now. This was the rainy season, they explained, and the torrential downpours of the past few weeks had caused the two rivers to swell so high that it was impossible to cross them except by swimming. And the water was full of crocodiles. Etc., etc....

Ill. 2.102

Native man holding a chameleon

Ill. 2.103

Ill. 2.104
Gorgeously colored conifer slice

I applied all my negotiating skills, exerted all my charm and promised exorbitant tips, but to no avail. Nothing could persuade the two local men to change their minds. Our disappointment was exacerbated by the fact that the petrified forest lay so tantalizingly close, but we had no other choice except to commence the long and strenuous journey back to Antananarivo. Perhaps we should have heeded the words of a Madagassy who, just twenty-four hours before we set out on our ill-fated expedition, had warned us that it would be absolutely impossible for us to reach the petrified forest during the rainy season (ill. 2.97, 2.98, 2.99). I spent a few days relaxing on the shores of the Indian Ocean, where my friend Robert and I celebrated Christmas together in a shack in the jungle (ill. 2.100). Civilization simply hadn't penetrated here: no television, no radio, no electric light, but our privations were amply compensated by the presence of five charming Madagassy ladies whose hospitality greatly contributed to our enjoyment of the few days we spent there (ill. 2.101). When we returned to Antananarivo, I met a retired German high-school teacher who promised to send me photographs of the petrified forest. And indeed, he kept his word.

### A Triassic Forest

The petrified forest of Madagascar is about 230-million-years old and is composed primarily of fossil conifers, most of which seem to have been araucarioid needle-bearing trees. The fact that this site has yielded no specimens of twigs or trunks with roots has led scientists to conclude that the trunks must have grown elsewhere and been deposited here by the ocean. The spectrum of colors is enormous. Along with brown, red, yellow and blue shades, it is not uncommon to find specimens displaying lovely greenish tints which suggest the presence of chromium dioxide (2.102, 2.103, 2.104). It is legal to remove petrified wood from Madagascar, but goods intended for export must be in a "worked condition," which means that you must have your specimens cut and polished before you attempt to carry them out of the country.

# AUSTRALIA

## The Petrified Forest of Queensland

Ulrich Dernbach

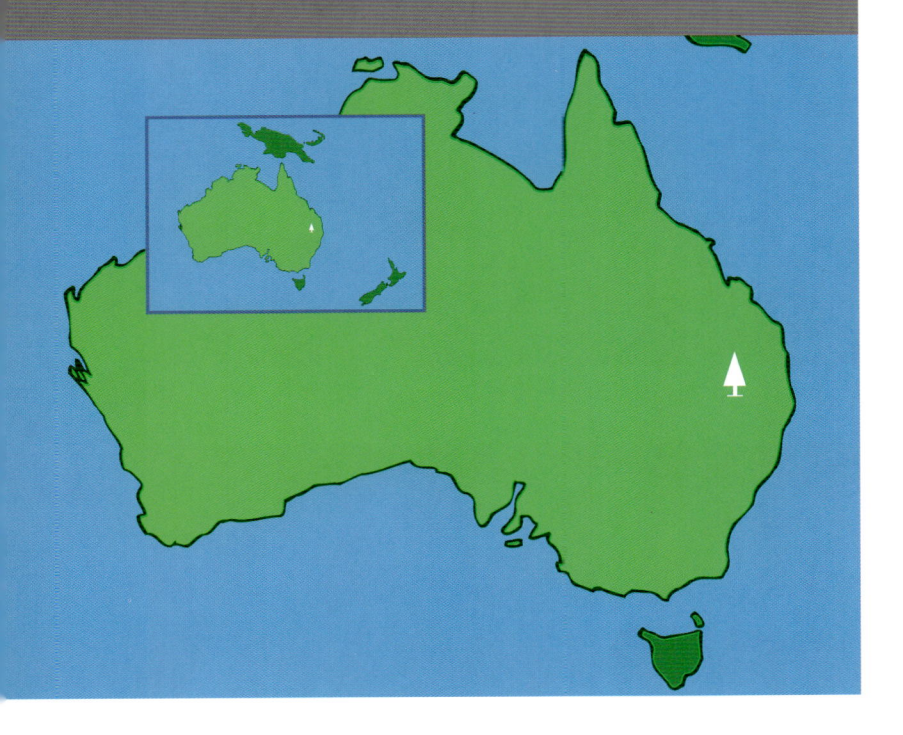

W hen the conversation turns to the petrified forests of Australia, most people immediately think of discovery sites in Queensland and Tasmania. This report will focus on those two sites.

Nevertheless, I should mention that there is also a considerable discovery site in northwestern Australia too. The petrified wood found here is called "peanutwood," so-called because it almost always shows the characteristic ovals left where *teredo* worms have eaten their way into the wood. Peanutwood is avidly sought by collectors (ill. 2.105).

This site lies 94 miles (150 km) east of Carnavon. The petrified trees here are Jurassic conifers.

Ill. 2.105

### Toowoomba

Australia's largest exhibition of minerals and fossils was held in Toowoomba, Queensland from April 5 to April 8, 1996. Since the most beautiful and most spectacular petrified woods are found in Queensland, I hoped to find some especially lovely collector's items at this mineral fair (ill. 2.106).

Ill. 2.106

Ill. 2.107 Norman Donpon

Ill. 2.108

My plane landed on schedule in Brisbane on April 4th. The next morning I rented a car and drove two hours to Toowoomba. I asked for directions to Australia's most important exhibition of minerals and fossils, and was pleased to discover that I was among the fair's first visitors. Nothing had been bought up ahead of me.

**Disappointment**

I had planned to spend two full days at this mineral fair; even in my worst nightmares, I never would have imagined that I could browse through every stand in a mere two hours. I ended up spending less than 20 dollars for a couple of small, unpolished slices of petrified wood.

Microscopic photograph, enlarged 32 times.

Ill. 2.109

97

Ill. 2.113  Microscopic photograph showing roots of an Osmundaceae, enlarged 54 times. Collection: Norman Donpon

### You Just Have to Be Lucky

Then, in the special show, I found the woods I'd come here to buy. But they weren't for sale; these were showpieces belonging to the collector Norman Donpon. As chance would have it, a few minutes later I was interested to a stranger who turned out to be none other Norman Donpon himself. He offered to accompany me to the petrified forest of Queensland the very next day, and was also eager to show me his own collection of petrified woods in Meandarra.

### How to Get There

The petrified forest of Queensland is located halfway between Toowoomba and Roma on Route 54, not far from the little towns of Chinchilla and Miles. A large number of araucarioid woods can still be found at the site today, but collectors should come prepared to dig (2.107).

Along with the araucarias (ill. 2.108, 2.109), some ferns (Osmundaceae) (ill. 2.110) and *Pentoxylon* (ill. 2.111) can also be found. The specimens are almost always "rolled," which means that they have been moved about and abraded by water action for a long time. Although scientific opinion has varied, most experts now agree that this forest dates from the Jurassic.

Abb. 2.112 Collection: Norman Donpon

Ill. 2.111
*Pentoxylon*,
Miles, Australia

## The Collection

After Norman Donpon showed me the major discovery sites in the petrified forest, we drove to Meandarra. A short time later, I was able to examine a remarkable collection. Norman allowed me to photograph some of his more uncommon pieces.

I was especially happy when he agreed to a swap, and I became the proud possessor of fern wood and *Pentoxylon*, both of which were duplicates in his collection (ill. 2.112, 2.113).

Thanks to Norman Donpon, my trip to Toowoomba proved eminently worthwhile after all!

Ill 2.110
Osmundaceae,
Lune River,
Australia.
Photo: Rod Hewer

# AUSTRALIA

# The Petrified Forest of Tasmania

Ulrich Dernbach

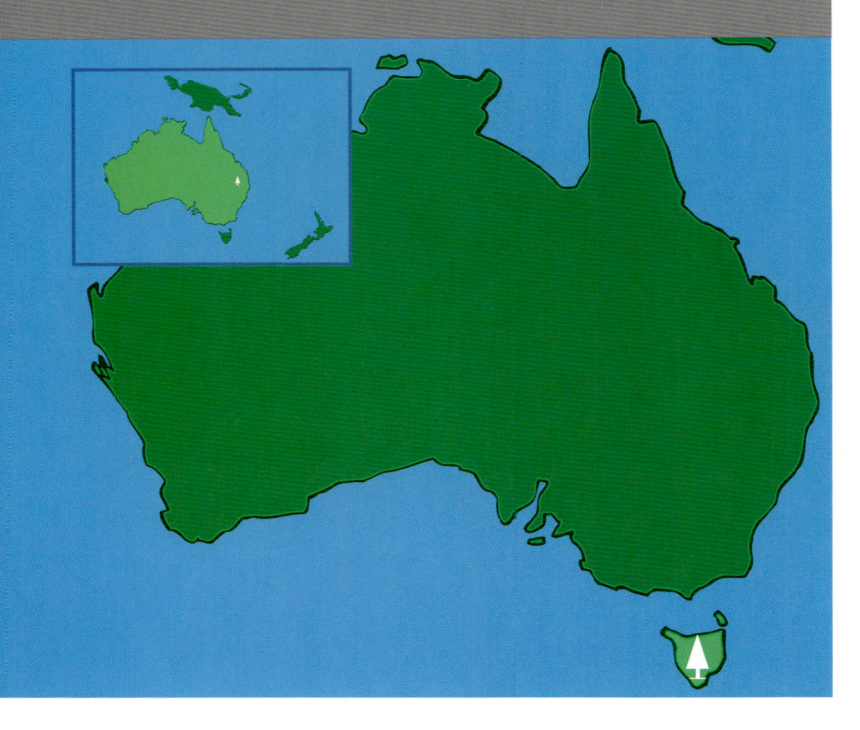

T he journey to Tasmania was another high point in my visit Down Under.

My flight left Melbourne on April 27, 1996, and after only an hour in the air, we prepared to land in Hobart, the capital of the island. I had already arranged to pay a visit to collector Ron Smythe, who lives in Hobart. When I arrived at his house, I was pleasantly surprised to find Ron waiting for me at the door.

**The Collection**

A short time later, Ron Smythe began to show me his impressive collection of fossilized woods. He told me that he and his friend Rod Hewer, whom I would meet the next day, were among the island's first collectors and that they were both founding members of the Tasmanian Palaeontological Union. A focal point of Ron's collection, and one which, of course, I found particularly interesting, are the gourgeously colored petrified ferns (Osmundaceae) found at Lune River. I photographed a few of the prettiest specimens, and improved my own collection by swapping a few of my specimens for some of Ron's petrifications (ill. 2.114, 2.115, 2.116).

I made plans to meet Rod Hewer early the next morning. He also owns a grand collection. Along with the excellent ferns, I was especially impressed by a marvelously patterned opalized oak from Bushy Park, Tasmania (ill. 2.117) and by a bright red araucarioid wood from Swansea, Tasmania (ill. 2.118). After allowing me to take a few photos, Rod offered to show me the discovery sites at Lune River.

Ill. 2.114

Ill. 2.115  Collection: Ron Smythe

Ill. 2.116  Collection: Rod Hewer

101

Ill. 2.117 Photo by and from the collection of Rod Hewer

### How To Get There
Drive south out of Hobart along Route A6, which follows the Huon River. Shortly before Southport, turn off A6 and drive toward Hastings. Signs will soon appear directing you to Lune River (ill. 2.119). From there, drive south on Catamaran Road (Route C636).

### The Petrified Forest
About 1,650 feet (500 m) farther on, we found ourselves in Tasmania's petrified forest. Rod explained that the now avidly sought fern wood was first discovered in 1962 by workers building a road. At the time, the find was misidentified as petrified palm wood. Only many years later were they recognized as Jurassic ferns (Osmuncaceae). Prof. Tidwell from the United States deserves much of the credit for this.

Ill. 2.118 Collection: Ron Smythe

Traces of the excavations dug by past fossil hunters can be seen on both sides of the road. Nevertheless, the site is by no means exhausted, and large reserves of fossils still await discovery beneath the rough and poorly accessible terrain. Bushes as tall as a man, and especially the

Ill. 2.119

Ill. 2.120
Rod Hewer and my wife: Two avid "fossil hunters"

razor-sharp leaves of the so-called "cutting grass" further impede one's passage (ill. 2.120). Rod also warned me to watch out for the many poisonous snakes, and advised me not to underestimate their danger. By the way, digging for and collecting petrified wood is permitted here, although the discovery of unusually large petrifications must be registered with the state.

# NEW ZEALAND

# The Petrified Forest of New Zealand

Mr. and Mrs. Ray, U.S.A.

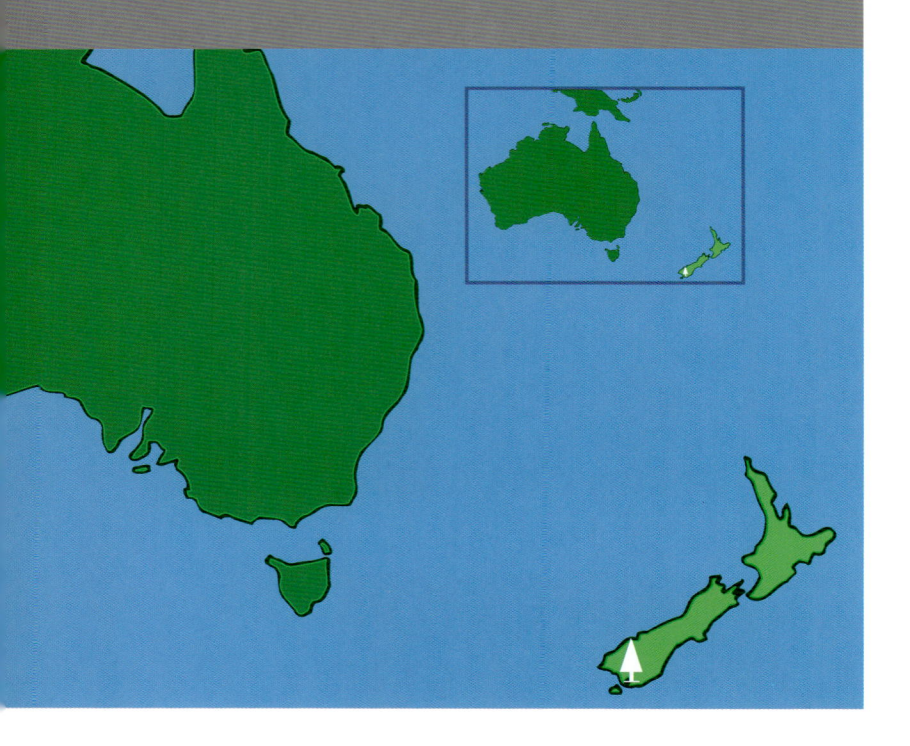

In the southernmost part of New Zealand you can visit a petrified forest which is most comfortably admired while wearing a bathing suit.

### How to Get There
Invercargill is the nearest town. It's just 20 miles (32 km) from here to Toetoes Bay, where you'll find signs leading you to the petrified forest at Curio Bay. Equally rewarding, however, is the drive to the forest from the lovely university town of Dunedin. The city has an interesting "wildlife area" where you can watch albatrosses and yellow-eyed penguins. A gorgeous, three-hour drive along Route 1 brings you directly into the petrified forest.

### The Eternal Ebb and Flow
If you arrive at this petrified forest at high tide, you'll see plenty of ocean, but no trees, because this fossil forest is only exposed at low tide (ill. 2.121). (Tide-tables and other essential information are available at Catlin Tourist.) But when the tide is low, you will enjoy unimpeded access to an area 0.6 mile (1 kilometer) in length and about 825 feet (250 m) in width where you can admire giant petrified trees, some of which measure as much as 99 feet (30 m) in length (ill. 2.122).

### The Jurassic
Scientists believe that this petrified forest was formed during the Jurassic period. Araucarioid coniferous trees flourished in this region about 160 million years ago.

If what signs posted in the park claim is true, then this sandbank has yielded specimens of Norfolk Island pines *(Araucaria heterophylla)*, as well as endemic Kauri pines *(Agathis australis)*.

### Warm Summers
A camping trip with a house trailer is definitely recommended. Warm summer weather makes relaxing at the nearby campgrounds and waiting for the tide to ebb a pleasant way to pass the time.

Ill. 2.121   The petrified forest at low tide

Cretaceous araucarioid trees

Ill. 2.122

105

# CHINA

# The Petrified Forest of Xinjiang

Guanghua Liu

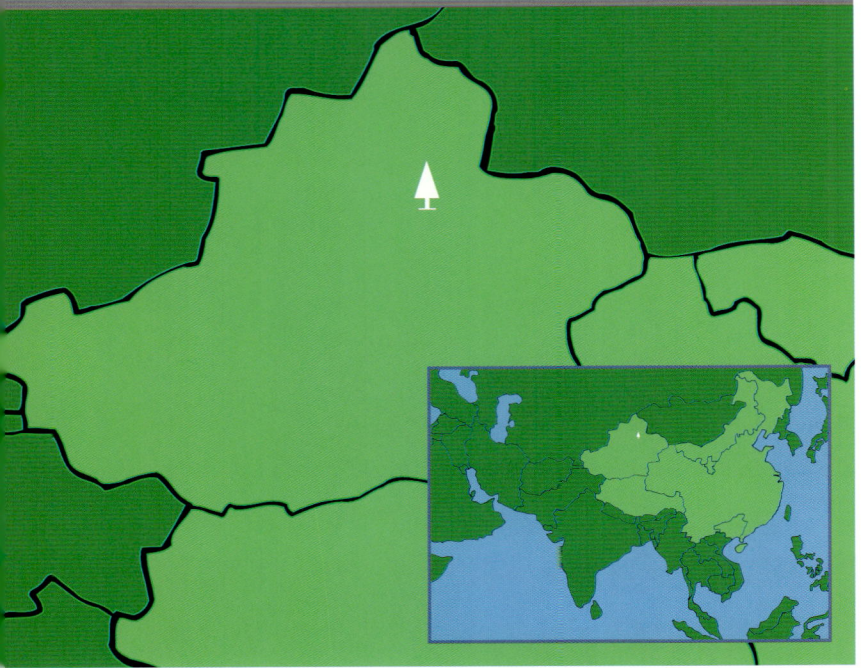

M any sites yielding petrified wood have been discovered in China.

The best known are located in the provinces of Henan, Shaanxi, Anhuai, Hubei, Beijing, Jiangxi and Xinjiang.

The oldest woods from these sites were petrified during the Carboniferous; the most recent specimens are a "mere" 10 million years old and date from the Tertiary. The external appearance of these grayish black petrifications is, unfortunately, not especially attractive.

## The Exception

There is, however, one beautifully colored petrified forest in China. It is located in Xinjiang Province, in the vicinity of Jimoshaer and Qitai.

Along with specimens of petrified conifers, fossil ferns (Osmundaceae) and horsetails have also been found. Spectacular discoveries of the fossilized dinosaur *Tienshansaurus chitaiensis* attracted a great deal of scholarly attention.

Dr. Guanghua Liu, who wrote this report, has concentrated on that portion of Xianjiang's petrified forest which lies in the Qitai region. All photographs in this chapter were taken there.

## How To Get There

As already mentioned, Xinjiang's petrified forest is found in the Jimosher region (in the northeastern portion of the Jungeer Depression) and in Qitai, the northern loop of the Tianshan mountain range.

## Qitai

The petrifications are found in Jiangjun Desert, about 94 miles (150 km) north of the city of Qitai. The forest here covers an area 5 miles (8 km) in length and 3.1 miles (5 km) in width.

Ill. 2.125

Ill. 2.123

Deciduous wood, Guangxi Province, China. Collection: H. Schmidt

Ill. 2.124

Conifer, Guangxi Province, China. Collection: H. Schmidt

The author counted a total of about 400 tree trunks, some of which had achieved gigantic sizes: 99-foot (30 m) long trunks are not a rarity, and many of them reach diameters in excess of 59 inches (1.50 m) (ill. 2.123, 2.124). But what makes this forest truly extraordinary is the fact that a large number of trunks are still standing upright (ill. 2.125; photo by G. Liu).

Chinese palaeontologists believe that Xinjiang's petrified forest dates from the Jurassic. Their anatomical research suggests that the majority of the relics are derived from a type of pine (*Pinus sp.*).

# BELGIUM

# The Petrified Forest at La Calamine

Henri Gielen

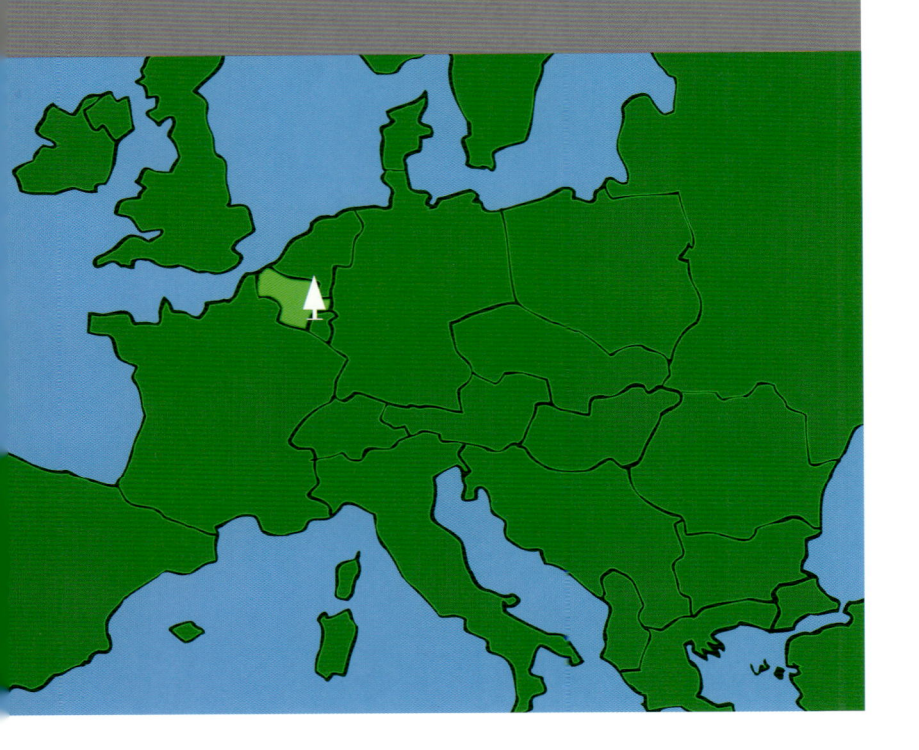

*Until a few years ago, petrified wood from La Calamine was seldom available. But there's a special reason to explain why every enthusiastic collector wants at least one specimen from this region.*

### How To Get There
The little Belgian town of La Calamine is located near the border with Germany and Holland, not far from Aachen.

### Zinc Ore
The region around La Calamine (Kelmis) has long been known for its zinc ores. In fact, it was this ore, which was mined intensively here during the 18th and 19th centuries, that gave the city its name (Lapis Calaminaris = Galmei).

**Right and left: Käskorb quarry and Hauset**

### The Petrified Forest
Numerous sand quarries are scattered throughout the La Calamine region, and with a little luck, you might find some attractive specimens of petrified wood in one of those excavations. A closer look at these specimens reveals that the smaller boughs and trunks are pierced through with variously sized tunnels, silent testimony to the appetite of the voracious shipworm *(Teredo navalis)*. These creatures, which are usually between 4 and 18 inches (10 and 45 cm) in length, posed a serious threat to the wooden hulls of 18th century sailing ships.

### Hauset and Käskorb
A remarkable variety of woods can be found in the abandoned pit at Hauset and especially in the still-active sand pit at Käskor (northeast of La Calamine). Large trunks have been discovered in both places. Lengths of 20 inches (50 cm) are not uncommon. If you have

Ill. 2.128

these woods cut and polished, you'll be rewarded with gorgeous collector's items. The petrifications frequently show lovely annual rings, and the shipworm tunnels are often filled with deep blue chalcedony. Some of these woods even reveal marvelous agates (ill. 2.128, 2.129).

### Cretaceous
These sand pits are the remains of sand dunes created during the Upper Cretaceous. At that time, this region was part of the Belgian-Dutch Cretaceous sea. The trunks found in the petrified forest at La Calamine are actually ancient and mostly coniferous driftwood, a fact which explains why shipworm tunnels are so frequently encountered.

Ill. 2.129
Coniferous wood with chalcedony

109

# GERMANY

# The Petrified Forest at Chemnitz

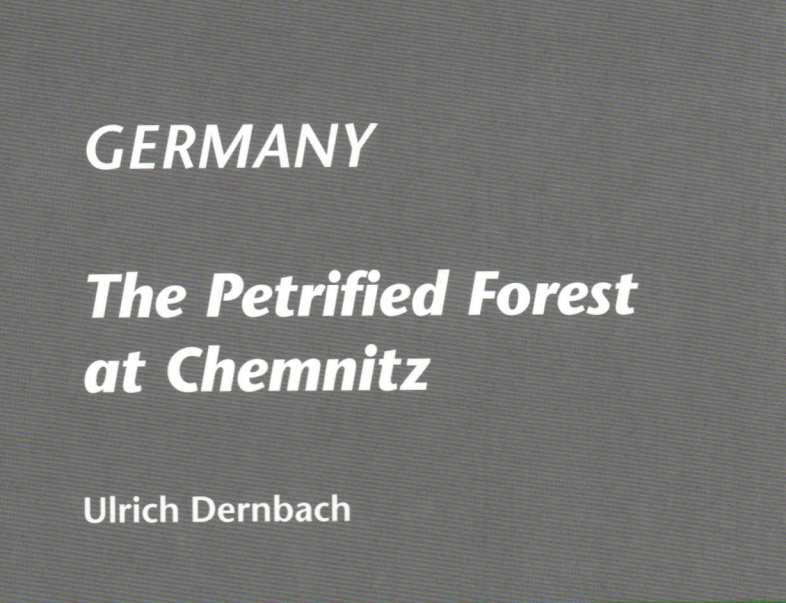

Ulrich Dernbach

Ill. 2.129

*Where can you find a petrified forest in the middle of major city? Did you guess Chemnitz, Germany? You're right: Chemnitz Petrified Forest.*

Ill. 2.128

### How to Get There

Chemnitz Petrified Forest is located where Autobahn E 62 intersects Autobahn E 63. You'll find this unique natural spectacle in the middle of the city, in the immediate vicinity of King Albert Museum. More than 30 giant petrified trees provide silent testimony to the fact that you are indeed standing in the midst of primordial forest (ill. 2.128, 2.129, 2.130, 2.131, 2.132).

### The 18th Century

During the 18th century, and as part of their tireless efforts to keep the city's treasury well filled, the Saxon archdukes appointed so-called "precious stone inspectors" and entrusted them with the twofold task of searching for semiprecious stones and other minerals that could be polished, and also making sure that the money generated through sales of those stones would be duly surrendered to the ruling noblemen.

David Frenzel was appointed "archducal gemstone inspector" in 1743 and granted the exclusive right to search for petrified wood. Polished specimens of petrified wood soon became no less popular than the lovely agates that were also found in this region. Especially beloved and correspondingly high-priced was the multicolored *starstein* (psaronius). This mineral derives its name from its similarity to the colorfully iridescent, speckled plumage of the

Ill. 2.130

starling. (*Star* is the German word for "starling" and *psaros* is Greek for "speckled.")

In the years following 1750, Frenzel excavated many wagon-loads of petrified wood and delivered them to polishers in Dresden. The majority of the finished wares were exported to foreign countries, especially to St. Petersburg in Russia.

### An Englishman

It didn't take long for people to realize that these petrified specimens were in fact the fossil remains of ancient trees, but precise identification was not yet

Ill. 2.131

Ill. 2.132

*Ill. 2.133*
*Dadoxylon*

possible at this date. Basing their hunches on superficial similarities alone, the petrifications were compared with modern endemic trees, mostly oaks and beeches. Not until the Englishman W. Nicol prepared the first thin sections in 1830 did it become possible to determine the specimens' true identities.

*Ill. 2.134*
*Dadoxylon*

### Heinrich Cotta

Anyone writing the history of Chemnitz Petrified Forest would be well advised not to forget one very important name: Heinrich Cotta, director of Saxony's forest survey office.

During his term in office, Cotta collected more than 500 trunks, which he sent for slicing and polishing. Diary entries prove that a few of these gorgeous specimens found their way into Goethe's mineral collection. The greater part of Cotta's marvelous collection, however, is now on display in Berlin at Humboldt University's Museum of Natural History (Museum für Naturkunde).

### Sterzeleanum

Many years of dedicated collaboration between Max Güldner, an architect and master builder from Hilbersdorf, and the already famous palaeobotanist Johann Traugott Sterzel brought Germany the distinction of possessing one of the world's foremost collections of minerals from the Lower Permian period. The combined efforts of these two men helped prevent collectors and gemstone hunters from absconding with silicified woods. The original collection that Güldner and Sterzel amassed now forms the cornerstone (no pun intended) of a remarkable collection bearing the name of its godfather: the "Sterzeleanum."

### 250 to 280 Million Years Ago

Plants and trees must have enjoyed excellent growing conditions in the Chemnitz Trough during the Lower Permian period (between 250 and 280 million years ago). In recent years, petrified specimens of approximately 80 different species of plants have been collected at several sites within the City of Chemnitz and in its suburb of

Ill. 2.135
*Psaronius*

**Cross-section of a *Psaronius* leaf**

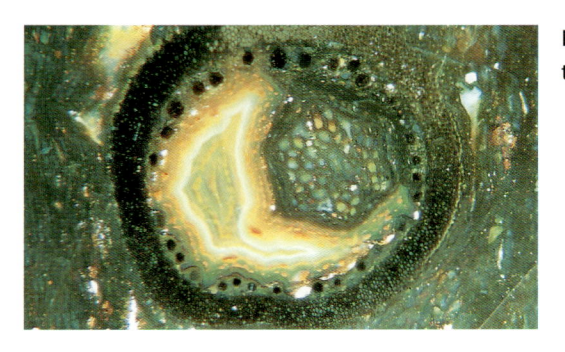

Enlarged 18 times

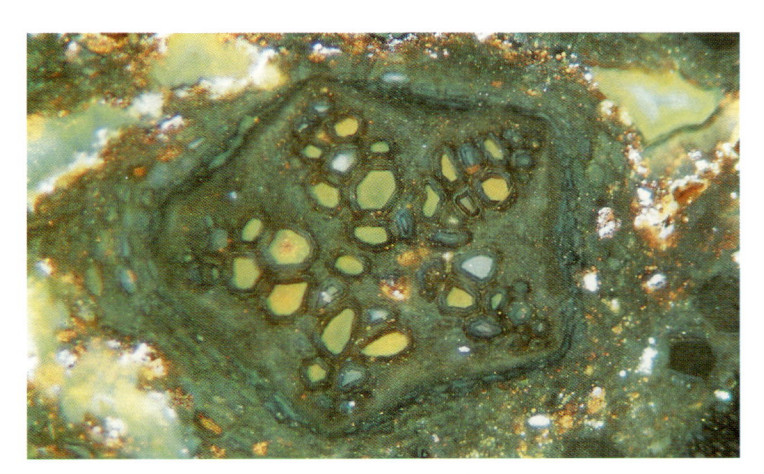

Aerial root of a *Psaronius,* enlarged 38 times.

### *Dadoxylon*

(Ill. 2.133, 2.134) The largest proportion of silicified trees are so-called *Dadoxylon* trunks. These specimens are the petrified trunks of Permian cordaites and araucarioid conifers. One 87-foot-long (26.3 meter-long) tree trunk was unearthed in Hilbersdorf in 1911. Today, visitors to this petrified forest can admire a massive, 17-foot-long (5.25-meter-long) petrified tree trunk.

### *Psaronius*

Thanks to their bright colors and distinctive structures, the most spectacular specimens come from ancient tree ferns *(Psaronius)*. A microscope or magnifying glass sometimes reveals gorgeously colored agates in the aerial roots. Most of these trunks were rather slender: though they attained heights of up to 40 feet (12 m), tree ferns seldom exceeded 13.7 inches (35 cm) in diameter (ill. 2.135, 2.136).

Hilbersdorf. Among the most spectacular discoveries are specimens of tree ferns, seed ferns, arboreal horsetails, Cordaites and conifers.

Ill. 2.136
*Psaronius sp.*
Collection of the Chemintz Museum of Natural History

## Plants in the Horsetail Group

These are some of the more simply structured plants in the petrified forest at Chemnitz. Palaeobotanists distinguish between two types of trunk: *Calamodendron* and *Arthropitys*. These primordial horsetails were as tall as trees: heights of more than 26 feet (8 m) and diameters up to 9.8 inches (25 cm) were not uncommon (ill. 2.137).

## *Medullosas*

Despite their fern-like appearance, the various species in the *Medullosa* genus are classed among the seed ferns. Unlike horsetails and true ferns, these plants reproduce by means of seeds. Long, unbroken specimens are quite rare, so it is impossible to say exactly how tall Permian *Medullosa* plants actually grew. Estimates based on measurements of mature trunks suggest that they may have reached heights of as much as 33 feet (10 m) (ill. 2.138).

Ill. 2.137
*Calamodendron*
Collection of the Chemintz Museum of Natural History

Ill. 2.138 *Medullosa*

## Afterword

In the recent past, and until shortly after the reunification of the two German nations, Dr. Kleinsteuber and his curator, geologist Gerald Urban, directed the natural history museum in Chemnitz. Despite their best efforts, these two men were unable to prevent the greater part of the Sterzel Collection from being packed into crates and hidden from public view.

Since then, however, the young geologist Dr. Ronny Rössler from Chemnitz has succeeded Dr. Kleinsteuber as director of the museum. We can only hope that this capable and industrious young man will be able to persuade the City of Chemnitz to provide him with sufficient funds and exhibition space so that the Sterzel Collection can once again be displayed and admired as a permanent exhibit.

Star-shaped ring of a *Medullosa,* enlarged 8 times

# Czech Republic

# The Petrified Forest of Nová Paka

Ulrich Dernbach

The petrified forest at Chemnitz is not the only remarkable Permian forest in Europe. A second one exists at Nová Paka, Czech Republic.

**How To Get There**
If you're coming from Prague, drive 25 miles (40 km) along Highway E 65 toward Mladá Boleslav, then turn off the highway and take Route 16 through J to Nová Paka.

Ill. 2.142 The museum in Nová Paka

**The Petrified Forest**
The petrified forest lies buried beneath the red-brown soil, scattered across a 6-mile (10-km) wide area. The most beautiful specimens have been found in Nová Paka, Lísek, Balka, Vrchovina, Studenec, Stará, Paka and . Between 250 and 280 million years ago, this region was forested with calamites, psaronias (ill. 2.139, 2.140) and stigmaries (ill. 2.141). *Medullosas* were present, but less common. It wasn't so very long ago (1953) that Nová Paka's longest araucaria trunk was unearthed. The silicified giant measures 27.4 feet (8.30 m) in length and has a diameter of 3 feet (0.90 m).

Ill. 2.142a Araucarioid wood

Ill. 2.139
*Psaronius sp.*

## Museum

Nova Paká's new museum was opened in May 1996. Visitors can admire numerous unique specimens, all of which are lovingly displayed in showcases. The excellent *Psaronia* petrifications are equal in quality to those found in Chemnitz, both in their degree of preservation and in their spectrum of colors. The museum is well worth a visit (ill. 2.142, 2.142a).

Ill. 2.140
*Psaronius sp.*

Ill. 2.141
*Stigmarie*

# GREECE

# The Petrified Forest of Lesbos

Ulrich Dernbach

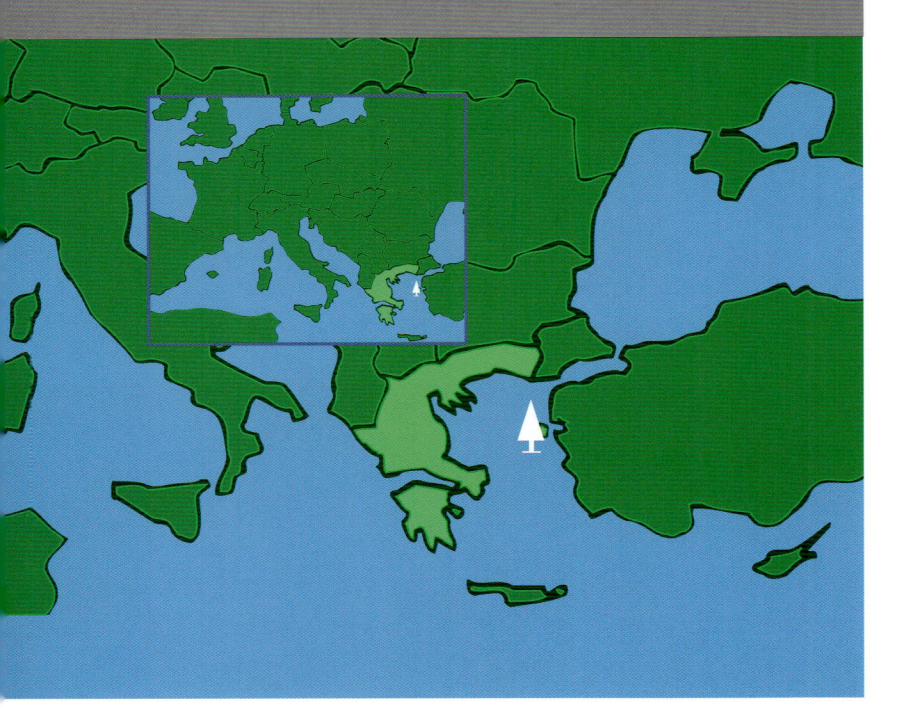

Would you like to take a special vacation to a place where you can enjoy culture, beaches, and a petrified forest? Go to Lesbos, Greece's third-largest island. Lesbos is located northeast of the Greek peninsula, within sight of the Turkish coast.

### How To Get There

Exactly 59 miles (94 km) separate the airport in the capital city of Mytilene from the village of Sikri in the western part of the island. About two hours' travel along a small and serpentine mountain road will bring you to this idyllic little fishing village (population 400).

### May 1994

The first time you come to Sikri to visit the petrified forest, it will probably be impossible for you to find all of the major discovery sites. I was lucky to have Herbert Schmidt as my guide. A German by birth, Schmidt loves the region and knows it well.

Timing our visit to Lesbos in mid-May turned out to be a wise decision. We enjoyed pleasant, early-summer temperatures (around 80° F / 25° C) all week long. And since there were few tourists this early in the season, we had the island virtually to ourselves.

### Five Sites or Five Forests?

There are five major sites for you to visit in the vicinity of Sikri. No one knows for certain whether these were once five discrete forests or merely the remnants of a single extensive forest.

Ill. 2.143 Wood from a coniferous tree

Ill. 2.144 Wood from a deciduous tree

Palaeontologists H. Süss and E. Velitzelos examined the specimens; R. Kräusel had already identified some of them years earlier. Most specimens are from conifers (ill. 2.143) of the type *Pinoxylon paradoxum* and *Taxodioxylon sp.*

Fossil deciduous trees (ill. 2.144) have since been discovered in the vicinity of Chamandrula near Eressos. According to Prof. Velitzelos, these specimens derive from ancient oaks, poplars, maples and palms.

All of these silicified woods date from the Tertiary, probably Oligocene or Lower Miocene.

Of the five sites on Lesbos, I'll describe only the three most important and, in my opinion, the most interesting ones. But for the sake of thoroughness, here's a list of all five sites:

- Pali Alonia
- The vicinity of Sikri
- Megalonissi (Nisiopi), a smal island about a mile (1.5 km) from Sikri
- Savakina
- Chamandrula near Eressos.

Ill. 2.145

Ill. 2.146

Ill. 2.148

### Pali Alonia National Park

The greatest collection of petrified wood is located about 9.4 miles (15 km) east of Sikri.

The trunks are found inside Pali Alonia National Park (ill. 2.145, 2.146). There are more than 100 trunks here, some of which extend between 6.5 and 10 feet (2 and 3 m) out of the ground. Their true length can only be guessed at. What makes this site so spectacular is the fact that the trees are still standing; on some of them, it's even possible to follow the petrified roots into the soil. Scientists are relatively certain that a natural disaster caused the silicification of this autochthonous petrified forest.

Plan to spend about an hour making a loop of the park. The hike is well worth your while, even though wire fencing spoils the view of some of these giant trees.

### The Sikri Vicinity

The 3.1-mile (5-km) walk from the village of Sikri to the lighthouse at Cape Sikri is a memorable experience. Again and again you'll encounter beautifully patterned land turtles, and in one little pond I counted no fewer than 75 water turtles.

A few hundred yards outside of the village, directly beside the sea, you'll find an astonishing sight: a 66-foot (20-m) long silicified trunk lies partly on land, partly in the water (ill. 2.147).

It isn't always easy to recognize the petrified tree trunks. Some are well camouflaged beneath the grass, others extend only a few inches above ground. In a few of these trunks, some of which were severely eroded, I was able to discern lovely annual rings; other specimens were gorgeously colored (ill. 2.148).

Ill. 2.147

**Megalonissi**

Don't miss an opportunity to visit the sensational discovery sites on this little island.

It takes about 15 minutes for the little boat to reach its dock. Arrange to meet your ferryman two hours later for the return voyage, thus giving yourself adequate time to see the sights at an unhurried pace.

The island can be divided into two halves: the hilly part features a chapel and a lighthouse; silicified wood is found on the more level (and more interesting) half.

At the outset of your stroll, a watchman will remind you of the severe penalties imposed for the theft of petrified wood. Be sure to obey the rules, because visitors will be carefully checked upon departure.

The stroll begins on the side of the island nearest the sea. Several small bays line the coast. A closer look into the crystal-clear water reveals numerous, sea-rounded petrifications. These colorful stones transform the sea floor into a shimmering mosaic of reds, blues and greens (ill. 2.149)

The island's chief attraction, however, is the following petrified forest. Descend a few steps toward the sea, and you won't believe your eyes:

Ill. 2.149

The view toward the petrified forest on the right-hand side of Megalonissi Island

Ill. 2.150

Ill. 2.151

Colossal silicified trees are lying in the midst of the ocean. Although they are whipped by waves day and night, these trees are in remarkably well-preserved condition (ill. 2.150, 2.151).

Also of interest are the petrified woods that extend out of the bay's volcanic bedrock. Some of these specimens display excellent annual rings.

After you've feasted your eyes here, follow the loop trail to the other side of the island.

Exercise caution crossing the island. We accidentally disturbed some breeding seagulls, who responded by diving precipitously toward us, only to veer off at the last instant, leaving their primate targets shaken but otherwise unscathed. Their display looked more dangerous than it actually was, but I was nonetheless relieved when I arrived safe and sound on the side of the island that faces Sikri.

A stroll along the gravel shore is worthwhile: here too you'll find a number of gigantic petrified trunks. We were able to follow the silicified roots of one especially impressive, upright stump for several yards until they disappeared into the surf.

Of course, we had spent longer than the planned two hours exploring the island, but a generous tip offered (and gladly accepted) again put us in the good graces of our ferryman.

# GREECE

# The Petrified Forest of Lemnos

Evagelos Velitzelos

Most reports about Greece's petrified woods refer only to the discovery sites on the island of Lesbos. But there is another petrified forest in Greece: on the island of Lemnos. This petrified forest is less well known because much of it lies within a restricted-access military reservation.

## Lemnos

Lemnos is small island located in the northern part of the Aegean Sea. With an area of 298 square miles (477 square km), Lemnos ranks among Greece's eight largest islands. It is easily reached by air from both Athens and Lesbos. A mere 90 miles (144 km) separate Lemnos from Lesbos.

Fishing harbor on Lemnos, Photo: Velitzelos

## The Petrified Forest

De Launay (1898) was the first person to mention Lemnos' petrified forest in print. Papp (1952), Berger (1953) and Velitzelos and Süss (1993) have also written about it.

I have made a dozen visits to this forest, and each time I see it, I am always astonished by its enormous dimensions. But it wasn't until my most recent visit (1996) that I discovered still-standing coniferous trees. The presence of vertical tree trunks proves that this forest, like the one on Lesbos, actually grew here before masses of lava covered it and led to its silicification.

## Discovery Sites

The best-known sites are located at Fergani, Moudros, Romanos, Varos, Roussopouli, and on the hill at Paradissi. Petrified trunks 6.6 to 10 feet (2 to 3 m) in length are not uncommon. Many of them are well preserved, although some others show the effects of severe weathering.

Ill. 2.152 Photo: Velitzelos

Ill. 2.154 Photo: Velitzelos

Ill. 2.153 Photo: Velitzelos

### Lesbos and Lemnos - Equally Old?

Scientists believe that the petrified woods found on both Lesbos and Lemnos are all about 20 million years old. It is therefore not surprising to find that the varieties of fossil plants and silicified trees on the one island are quite similar to those found on its neighbor. Twenty million years ago, the climate of the region is believed to have been tropical or subtropical; at this time, tremendous coniferous forests covered both islands.

Recent research on thin sections cut from petrified woods from these islands prove that most of these trees were sequoias (*Taxodioxylon gypsaceum*), cedars (*Cedroxylon sp.*) and pines (*Pinoxylon*) (ill. 2.152).

One difference between the Lemnos forest and that found on Lesbos is the presence of petrified palms on Lemnos. Fossil palms with extremely well-developed root mantles can be found in the Moudros vicinity. Specimens in such an excellent state of preservation are seldom encountered elsewhere (ill. 2.153, 2.154).

# TURKEY

## The Petrified Forest at Istanbul

Ulrich Dernbach

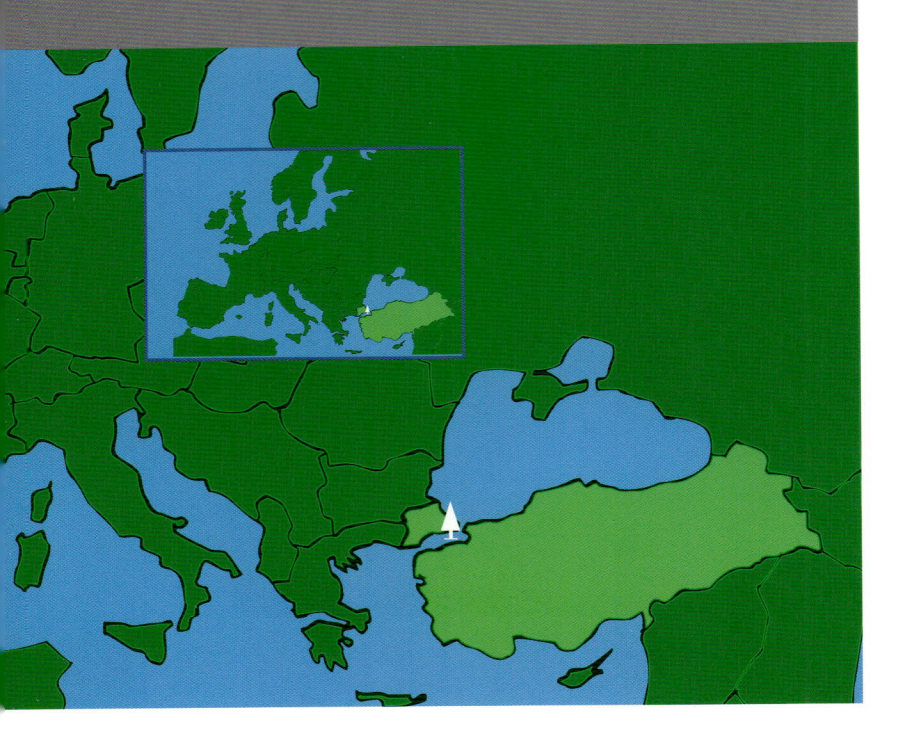

*I met a young Turkish fellow named Vedat Pisirici at the Munich Mineral Days Fair in 1995.*

*He told me that a petrified forest with opalized woods could be found near Istanbul, and then went on to say that he would be delighted to take me there.*

I landed at Istanbul Airport in January 1996, where I found Vedat waiting for me. We agreed to visit the petrified forest the very next morning.

**How to Get There**
Outside Istanbul, only a few miles from the airport, you'll find an area where many new dwellings have been built. Follow an unpaved road for a few hundred meters and you'll reach the site of the petrified forest, where you have a chance to find petrified wood scattered across an area measuring several square kilometers. Unfortunately, your discoveries are likely to be few and far between because over the past few years the majority of petrified branches and trunks have been carried off by collectors. Vedat assured me, however, that large quantities of colorful opalized wood still await discovery underground. I discovered several small trunks, some of them in perfect condition, which featured lovely red, blue and green colors (ill. 1.155, 1.156, 1.157). I also found a series of variously sized woods in a sandy, several-meters-tall slope nearby.

**Opalized wood**

Ill. 2.155 Opalized wood

Ill. 2.156
Opalized wood

Ill. 2.158
The "wonder-working" trunk

### Mysterious Powers

The largest and most spectacular specimen, however, was found some years ago. Just a few miles from here, villagers discovered a massive, 5-foot (1.5-m) long and 27-inch (70-cm) thick trunk. News of the discovery spread rapidly throughout the vicinity, and many people made the pilgrimage to admire the fossil (ill. 2.158).

Some local residents believe that the trunk possesses mysterious powers, which explains why so many people stricken with illness or bad luck make the pilgrimage, hoping that the magical stone will relieve their suffering.

### Deciduous and Coniferous Trees

When I returned to Germany, I learned that the specimens were derived from deciduous and coniferous trees of the Tertiary period. Thin sections have not yet been prepared, so it is still impossible to determine precisely which species of trees were petrified here.

Ill. 2.157 Opalized wood

# TURKEY

# The Petrified Forest at Ankara

Ulrich Dernbach

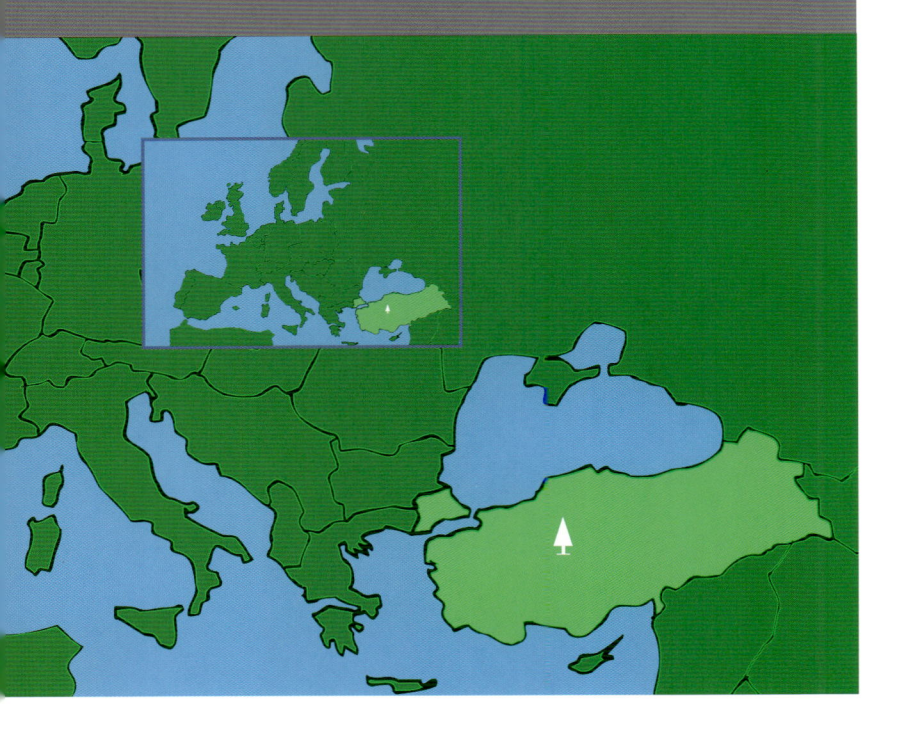

I received a mysterious telefax from a Turkish businessman one day in January 1994. He wrote that he was the owner of a petrified forest and had heard that I was writing a book about such forests. He closed his telefax by inviting me to visit him and his forest in Ankara.

### How to Get There
Drive along Route E 90 from Ankara toward Istanbul for about 94 miles (70 km), then leave the highway and head into the Kizilcahaman region. Here you'll find the petrified forest.

### A Hoax?
After phoning Turkey to assure myself that the fax was not merely a practical joke, I decided to accept Ali Iper's invitation. I arrived in Turkey in March 1994, where I met Iper, the forest's owner, in Ankara. After a moderate supper (without alcohol because of the Ramadan holidays) we arranged to visit the forest early the next morning. Temperatures that night dipped below freezing, but when I awoke the following morning I was pleased to see the sun shining brightly.

### At the Petrified Forest
We reached the petrified forest after about an hour's drive. Ali Iper's private forest occupies about 0.8 square miles (2 square km) of land not far from a little village. As we hiked across the hilly landscape with its numerous juniper bushes, I almost felt as if I were in Provence, southern France, rather than in Anatolia. Everywhere I looked, the ground was strewn with fragments of petrified wood, interspersed with an occasional twig or small branch. The density and number of specimens increased as we climbed the hill. Trunks up to 12 inches (30 cm) in length with diameters of about 8 inches (20 cm) were not uncommon. Some petrifications were only partly exposed by weathering: still half-buried, their exposed portions were shrouded in a layer of chalk.

Ali Iper, owner of the petrified forest

**The landscape as seen from the petrified forest**

**The author in his favorite environment**

Ali Iper explained that tons of petrified wood still lay hidden beneath the soil. To prove his claim, he asked two workmen to start digging. Within half an hour's time they had unearthed 33 variously sized fragments of branches and trunks. Here again, all of these petrifications were encased within a coating of white chalk.

Both Iper and a geologist who had accompanied us assured me that no scientific literature had yet been published about this petrified forest. For this reason, both the age and the botanical identity of the petrified woods were still unknown.

I solved the mystery a few months later when I learned that the woods found in the petrified forest at Ankara are mostly derived from conifers, especially juniper (ill. 2.159) and a particular species of Tertiary cypress (ill. 2.160).

I'll never forget that March weekend in Ankara. I was especially pleased and impressed by the cordial hospitality and generosity extended to me by my host Ali Iper and his son Bülent Iper.

Cypress in a coat of white chalk

Ill. 2.159
Juniper

Ill. 2.160
Cypress

**Abb. 3.3** Recent *Araucaria*

# The Tree

Rafael Herbst

There's an old saying, "You couldn't see the forest for the trees." And indeed, trees are the most important elements in any forest, including fossilized forests. It therefore seems pertinent for us briefly to discuss the phenomenon "tree."

## What is a Tree?

Everyone thinks they know what a tree is, but when we try to define it more precisely, we discover that the question is not so easily answered. Even botanists have several definitions to offer. We'll start with two examples. Some botanists claim that the chief difference between trees and shrubs lies in the superior height of the former; others emphasize the differences in branching. For our purposes, I would propose that we define a tree as "a woody plant with a well-formed trunk or bole and a more or less ramified crown of leaves or leaf-bearing branches." This definition is broad enough to include plants like the lepidodendrons and calamites of the Carboniferous, as well as the tree ferns, cycads, palms and conifers, together with a wide array of recent flowering plants. Trees range in size from the tiny Japanese bonsai trees to the towering (396 ft / 120 m) North American sequoias.

## The Structure

Since a woody plant body is characterized not only by its vascular and supportive tissues, but also by the arrangement of other tissues, it is necessary for us to examine the individual types of tissue in greater detail. For simplicity's sake we can identify two basic types of tissue within a woody body. On the one hand, certain tissues exist whose primary roles are associated with structural support and with the transport of water or nutrients. On the other hand, other types of tissue primarily serve storage purposes. With regard to this first kind of tissue, I will mention only the xylem elements (tracheids) and schlerenchyma (fibers), as well as (in modern plants), the fibers. A variety of more or less thin-walled parenchymatic tissues can be found within tissues that perform storage functions. Storage tissues play a relatively subordinate role in the identification of fossil woods, primarily because these tissues are seldom well preserved.

## Evolution

Tree-like organisms first arose in the plant kingdom during the Devonian period some 370 million years ago. Once arisen, the tree structure underwent a nearly explosive phase of evolution. This rapid flourishing can only mean that the tree is a highly successful type of structure for a plant, although it does have certain disadvantages compared to the structures evolved by shrubs and herbs. Chief among these disadvantages is the fact that a tree must use more energy to build its structure than is required to build the tissues and cells of a shrub or herb.

## Tree Types

Let us now consider the arrangement of the various tissues within the body of the tree. Nature has brought forth three main types, although many modifications have evolved within each type. We must not forget that the arrangement of the tissue must enable the tree to stand on its own, and must also make the tree sturdy enough to cope with external environmental factors like wind and weather.

**Type 1:**

A well-developed pith occupies the central area; the pithy center is surrounded by concentric bands of variously structured woody bodies.

Examples: lepidodendrons, calamites, cordaites and cycadophytes. Secondary xylem is usually an imporant component of this type, but is not always present in every case.

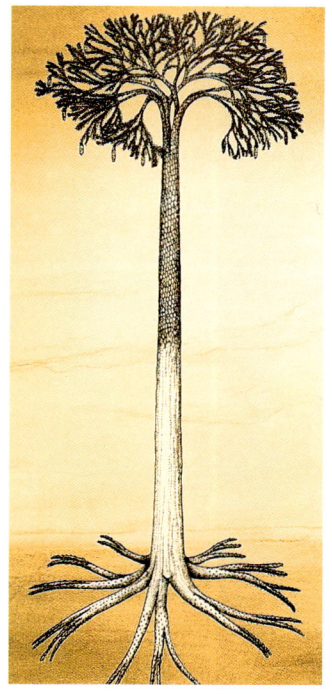

Ill. 3.1
Classical reconstruction of a lepidodendron.

**Type 2:**

A large number of more or less isolated, individual bundles are arranged above the cross-section of the trunk.

Examples: ferns, *Medullosas*, palms and arboreal cacti. Secondary xylem is usually lacking. Woody fibers take the place of secondary xylem.

Ill. 3.2
Reconstruction of a *Psaronius*

**Type 3:**

Pith is scarcely developed; concentric rings of constantly renewed, densely clustered secondary wood occupy nearly the entire cross-section of the trunk. This is the type of construction typically found in conifers and in most angiosperms. Tracheids are mostly confined to the angiosperms, where they appear as elongated xylem cells that lack lateral walls and aid in the transport of water. This structural type, characterized by clearly visible growth rings, is the sort of image one generally has in mind when seeks to define the word "tree" (ill. 3.3).

# Identification of Petrified Wood Made Easy

**Alfred Selmeier**

Many private collectors own polished slices of petrified wood. Fascinating colors, accompanying minerals and unique structures become visible when petrified tree trunks are cut and polished. But the question inevitably arises: To which type of wood or to which group of plants does a polished slice of trunk belong? In most cases, the naked eye or a magnifying glass suffices to identify slices of petrified trunks. The following article will offer some basic guidelines to assist collectors in assigning their polished specimens of petrified wood to the major botanical groups. More precise identification would require preparation of thin slides and intensive study of specialized scientific literature.

Ill. 4.1
Permian
*Lepidophyte*,
Nová Paka

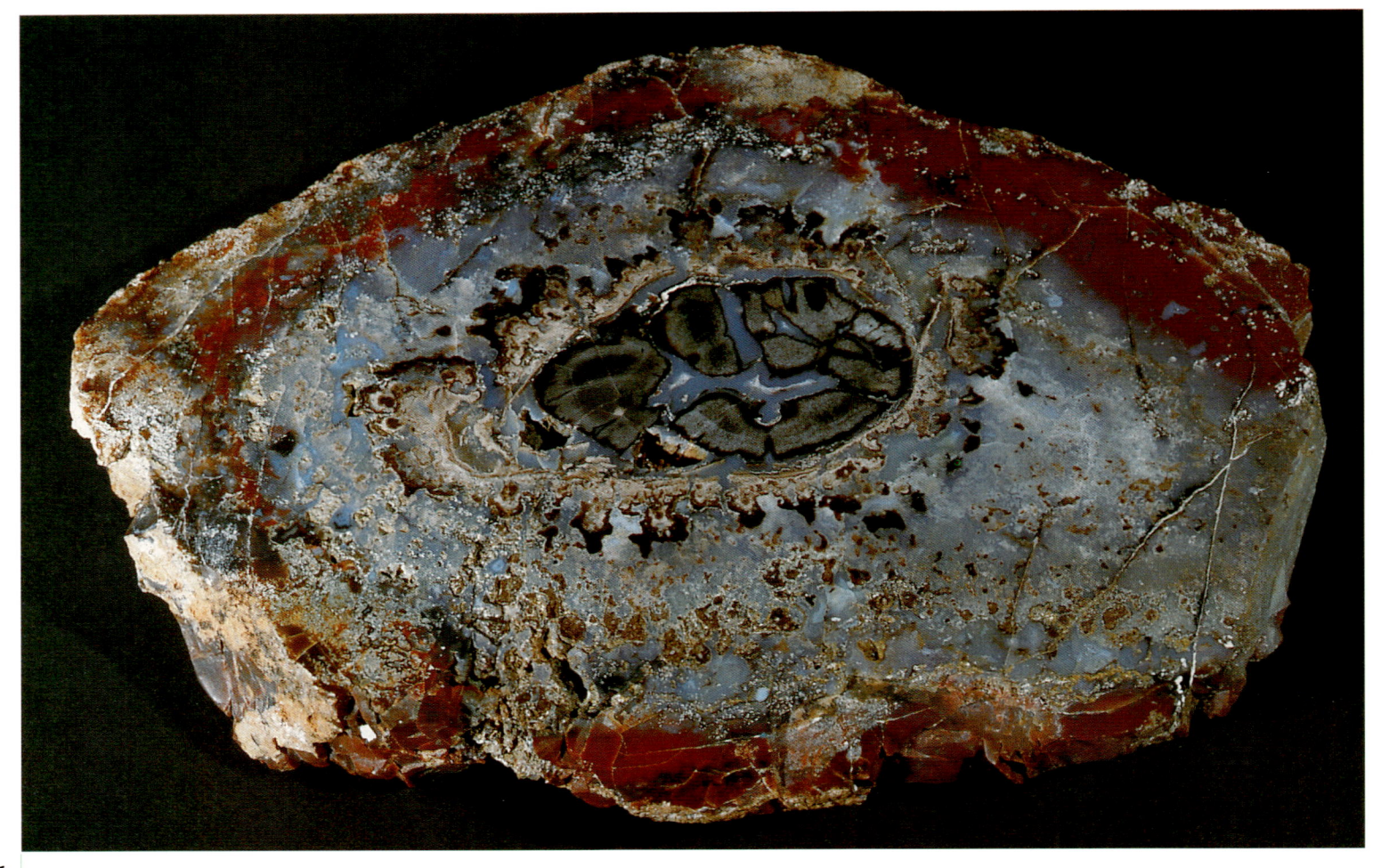

## The Word "Wood"

In everyday language, the inclusive term "wood" is used rather loosely to describe material derived from trunks, branches and roots. But if one investigates plant tissue more closely with the aid of a visible-light microscope, it soon becomes apparent that, in the more precise terminology of the botanical sciences, the term "wood" (Greek: *xylem*) really only refers to one highly specialized portion of the tissue within a particular plant. One ought therefore to exercise caution when using the term "wood" (xylem). In the following article, the word "wood" will be used only in its narrower, botanical sense. Xylem (wood) cells are formed in a layer of active cells called the "cambium." After their production in the cambium, newly formed xylem cells are generally released toward the inside of the plant. This process creates radially oriented rows of xylem cells which are easily seen when a polished specimen is viewed under a hand lens. This seasonal production of xylem cells causes trees to expand in girth. Known as "secondary thickening," this growth in girth is the combined result of the cyclical production of xylem cells complemented by formation of bark. The intensity of cell fission in the cambium varies periodically in response to environmental and climatic factors. In general, the cambium is active during the summer and dormant during the winter.

## Wood - Not Only from Recent Trees

Wood tissue (xylem) is commonly found in the familiar needle-bearing and deciduous trees of our present day and age. But polished slices of petrified trunks from the Palaeozoic and Mesozoic eras can also contain xylem cells. A magnifying glass is all one needs to recognize the presence of petrified woody tissue. In most cases, one finds radially oriented rows of cells, not unlike the pattern of stitches in a knitted sweater. Throughout a tree's lifetime, its woody tissues provide it with structural strength while serving as pipelines for the transport of water and nutrient salts. Together with other components of the trunk, woody tissue has been performing these essential functions ever since plants first emerged onto dry land. For millions of years, xylem has served as the plants' anatomical solution to the technical problems posed by gravity, providing plants with elastic rigidity and a means of transporting water upward. Nearly all plant groups that evolved vertical trunks (trees) have used xylem tissue to stabilize their upright stalks. Major groups include: arboreal lycopods (trees belonging to the genera *Lepidodendron* and *Sigillaria*), arboreal horsetails (Calamites), tree ferns (e.g., *Psaronius*), Cordaites, palm ferns, as well as the familiar needle-bearing and deciduous trees.

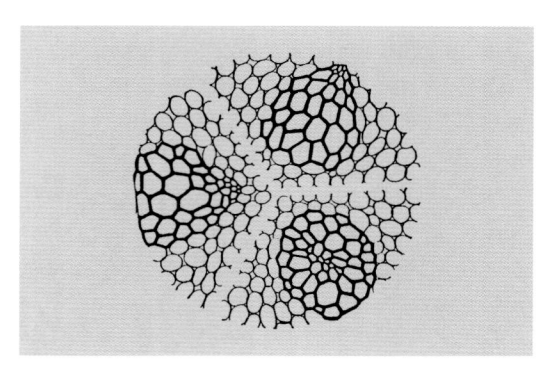

Ill. 4.2 Protostele: the arrangement of the small-celled protxylem can be either central, exarchic or endarchic

## Vascular Bundles and Sprout Axis

Familiarity with the major types of vascular bundles is essential for identifying polished slices of trunk. Brief information about the various types of vascular bundles will be useful to every collector of polished trunk slices. Anatomically, transverse sections of petrified "wood" from the Palaeozoic and Mesozoic eras are only somewhat comparable to woods from our modern needle-bearing and deciduous trees. Depending upon the geological era from which it is derived, a polished trunk slice may be built from one of several different types of "compound systems" involving various combinations of medulla (pith), xylem, bark, leaf-trace bundle and root-mantle. If the collector can identify the type of vascular bundle in a polished transverse section, then in many cases it becomes possible to localize the specimen within a preliminary botanical delimitation of possible plant groups. Botanists use the term "stele" (from the Greek word *stele*, column), to describe all varieties of vascular bundles, together with the pith and bark, within a given sprout axis.

"Protostele" (ill. 4.2) is a central, concentric vascular bundle, usually with interior xylem. The protostele is believed to be especially ancient and was a typical feature of the oldest land plants (e.g., *Rhynia*).

"Actinostele" (ill 4.3) is a central vascular bundle whose xylem appears star-shaped

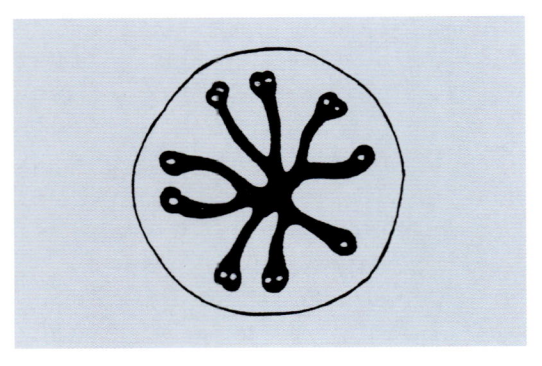

Ill. 4.3 Actinostele: in cross-section, the xylem shows a star-shaped arrangement

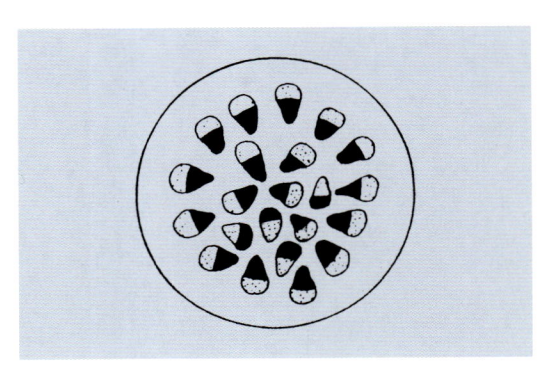

Ill. 4.5 Atactostele: in cross-section, the enclosed vascular bundles seem to be scattered at random

in cross-section. The term is derived from the Greek word *actinotós*, which means "surrounded by rays." Phloem is found between the rays of star-shaped xylem. Actinosteles are found in primordial ferns and in extant lycopods.

"Polysteles" are vascular bundles whose longitudinal axes are parallel to one other and evenly distributed throughout the entire cross-section of the sprout. The polystele is believed to have evolved from the actinostele as fissures along the actinostele's longitudinal axis became progressively deeper.

"Plectostele" describes a vascular bundle which appears braided when viewed in cross-section. The term is derived from

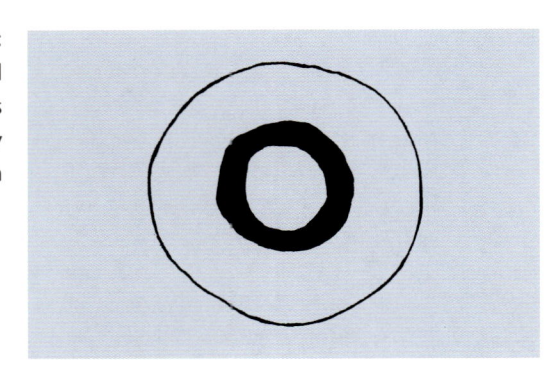

Ill. 4.4 Eustele: the enclosed pith is surrounded by a ring of xylem

the Greek word *plectós*, which means "braided." Plectosteles are the most common type of stele in the lycopod group.

"Siphonostele" denotes a tube-shaped strand of vascular bundles with central pith. The term is derived from the Greek word *síphon*, which means "tube." The siphonostele is very similar to the dictyostele.

"Dictyostele" is a net-like, interrupted tube of vascular bundles with leaf-trace strands. The term is derived from the Greek word *díctyon*, which means "net." It is typical of ferns.

"Eustele" (ill. 4.4): In general, the eustele corresponds to a concentric vascular bundle with enclosed pith. Eusteles are characteristic of calamites, conifers and angiosperms.

"Atactostele" (ill. 4.5): Atactosteles appear as self-contained, individual bundles randomly distributed across the entire cross-section of the slice. (Greek *átaktos*, "disordered"). Atactosteles are typical of monocotolydenous plants (e.g., palms) and the leaf stalks of seed ferns (e.g., the various species of *Medullosa*).

## Lycopod Plants

The best-known lycopods (Lycopodiopsida) are also called lepidodendron or sigillaria (ill. 4.6). Rich in both species and individuals, these genera (ill. 4.1) had a central pith with xylem cells (true wood), although these pith and xylem cells comprised only a very small percentage of the trunk's entire diameter. It seems that secondary xylem had not yet come to play a significant role in these trees' water transport or stabilizing functions. These so-called "bark trees" (ill. 4.7) derived their structural stability from the strengthening tissue found in their massively developed secondary bark. Sclerenchymatous cells

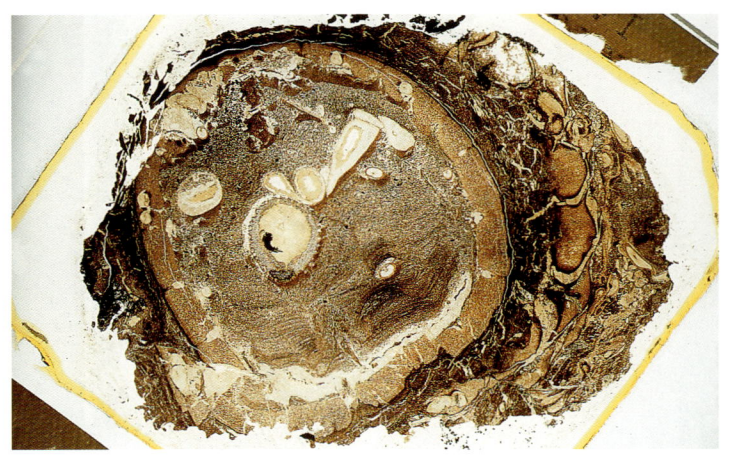

Ill. 4.6 Transverse section of Carboniferous *Lepidophlolos harcourii*, Littleborough, England; State Collection, Munich; photo: R.R. Rosin

within this massive bark served as the essential weight-bearing components for strengthening these trees' trunks. This type of trunk construction is unique in the evolutionary record. In the genus

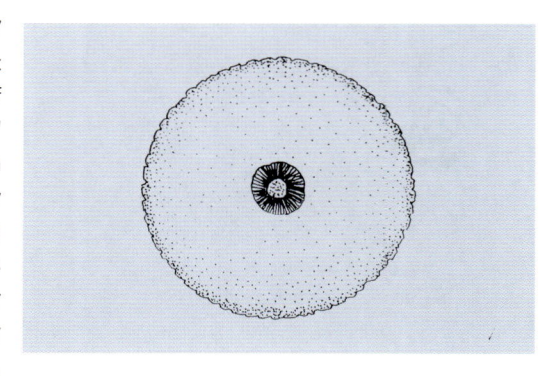

Ill. 4.7 Schematic cross-section of a "bark-stem." The small pith surrounded by a narrow ring of wood lies in the center of the thickly developed bark.

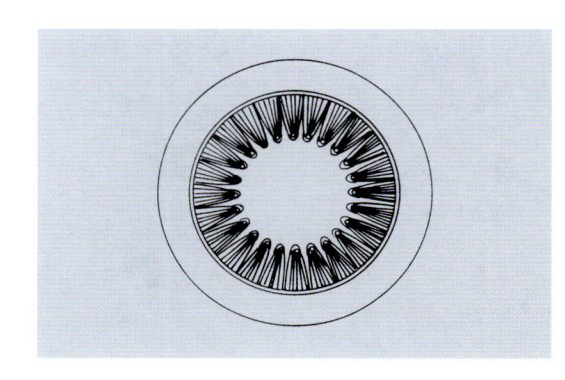

Ill. 4.9 Schematic cross-section of a "pith-stem." The large pith or large ring of wood is surrounded by centrifugal secondary wood. Small carinal cavities (in white) replace the destroyed primary xylem.

*Lepidodendron*, for example, bark accounts for 98% of the cross-section. As among nearly all Carboniferous-period plants of the northern hemisphere, here too annual rings and bordered pits are both absent. An active ring of cambium and partly single-rowed medullary (pith) rays suggest similarities to the woods found in modern conifers. The term "medullary ray," "pith ray" or "wood ray" is justified because the radially running rays of these "bark trees" extend all the way into the pith. In cross-section, the trunk's anatomy is : a) small central pith; b) xylem ring with medullary rays; c) massively developed primary bark with phelloderm.

## Horsetail Plants

Compared to the "bark trunks" of the arboreal lycopods, a markedly different construction arose among the calamites (ill. 4.8) during the Palaeozoic era, namely the various types of horsetails (Equisetopsida). Arboreal horsetail plants likewise belonged to the characteristic flora of Carboniferous forests. Some reached heights of 100 feet (30 m). Massive formation of secondary wood enabled these trees to attain diameters up to 39 inches (1 m). A large, central, medullary cavity ("pith stem") (ill. 4.9) formed the interior of this extinct type of trunk construction. True primary roots were probably absent, but the trees anchored themselves to the soil with prostrate rhizomes (underground stems). Each monopodial trunk grew upward in a telescoping fashion from one internodium to the next; this type of construction is still found in extant horsetails (*Equisetum sp.*). The extremely large pith is believed to be a "negative" function or "dead end" in plant evolution. This type of trunk construction follows the tubular principle,

Ill. 4.8 Permian calamite, Nová Paka

whereby mechanically important elements (xylem, bark) are placed on the outside, i.e., near the periphery. In cross-section, the trunk's anatomy is: a) pith and/or medullary cavity; b) primary wood with protoxylem and metaxylem; c) centrifugally developed secondary wood; d) medullary rays; e) narrow cribriform part; f) bark. The anatomical structure of the xylem, and especially the tracheid structure, are very similar to coniferous. This coniferoid structure of calamites trunks is a remarkable example of convergent evolution: though superficially similar, horsetails and conifers are botanically unrelated. Today's horsetails are fascinating Palaeozoic relics.

## Tree Ferns

Ferns endowed with tall, tree-like trunks (e.g., *Psaronius*) (ill. 4.12) evolved during the Carboniferous and Lower Permian periods. Immature tree ferns still have protosteles, but as the tree fern matures, its trunk increases in girth and its protosteles gradually change into dictyosteles. Curving, band-shaped vascular bundles are arranged in several rows and embedded within a central basic tissue. Seen in cross-section, one usually finds a rather complicated pattern of distribution of these band-shaped bundles at the center of the slice. So-called "leaf-bases" (ill. 4.11) located toward the sprout's periphery provide the central sprout axis with mechanical stability. A prominent abcission scar remains on the tree's trunk at the basis of each leaf after the leaves (fronds) have fallen off. Tree ferns derive additional stabilty from a massive mantle of sprout-borne root plexus. These sprout-borne adventitious roots grow along the trunk and penetrate the thick armor of the leaf-bases. Petrified tree ferns are avidly sought by collectors. These petrified "leaf-root trunks" should not be confused with petrified "wood" trunks. Even without a magnifying glass, polished slices of tree ferns (e.g., various species of *Psaronia*) can be distinguished from true petrified wood by examining their compound systems (vascular bundles, leaf-bases, root-mantles). Some specimens of *Psaronia* show only individual portions of the root-mantle or leaf-base. Brightly colored, silicified, polished cross-

Ill. 4.10 Part of an adventituous root from a Permian *Psaronius*, Chemnitz

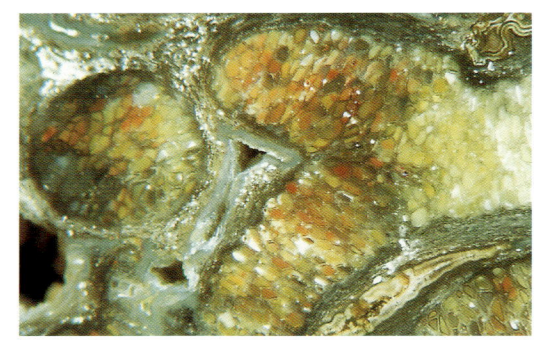

Ill. 4.11 Part of the leaf base from a Permian *Psaronius*, Chemnitz; enlarged 14 times

Ill. 4.12 Permian *Psaronius*, Chemnitz

Leaf bases and aerial roots; enlarged 10 times

Ill. 4.13 Cretaceous *Tempskya*, Oregon

sections of trunk (with paler, star-shaped, root vascular bundles) recall the brightly colored speckles in the iridescent plumage of various species of starlings. Frequently very beautiful when polished, these petrifications are known as asterolite, psarolite, psaronius ("speckled-stone" or "starling-stone"), eye agate (or Aleppo stone) and wormstone (so-called because of the worm-like appearance of the vascular bundles in the center of the trunk slice).

In cross-section and somewhat simplified, the trunk's anatomy is: a) central basic tissue; b) xylem with band-shaped vascular bundles curving convexly outward and embedded within the basic tissue; c) massive exterior zone with frond bases and aerial roots; d) exterior ring of sclerenchyma separating aerenchyma from denser tissue.

Not unlike the various species of *Psaronia*, the fossil osmundales also had a "leaf-root-trunk." Stele construction among the osmundales is unique and diverse.

There are several interpretations of the phylogenetic evolution of this type of stele structure among Palaeozoic and more recent osmundales. Tree trunks from the oldest fossil osmundales have a self-contained, central woody body or several more or less clearly defined siphonosteles (Zimmermann 1959). In cross-section and somewhat simplified, the trunk's anatomy is: a) inner, thin-walled xylem; b) inner bark with leaf traces and root traces; c) outer, thick-walled xylem; d) sclerenchyma ring of the outer tree bark; e) roots; f) inner and outer parenchyma.

## Cordaites

Cordaites (Cordaitopsida) flourished together with *Sigallaria, Lepidendron* and arboreal horsetails to form extensive Palaeozoic forests. Cordaites trees usually had slender, smooth, woody trunks and grew to heights of approximately 30 meters. They were the most highly evolved plants of Carboniferous-period forests. Grand'Eury (1877) found Cordaites trunks standing vertically in the stone quarries at St. Etienne. These petrified trees were still rooted in the ground. The anatomical structure of the petrified trunks is known in great detail. In cross-section and somewhat simplified, the trunk's anatomy is: a) massive, horizontally fan-like pith; b) primary xylem; c) secondary xylem; d) cambium; e) bark. Primary wood is composed of spiral tracheids and laddered tracheids; secondary wood shows araucarioid pitting on the radial walls. The term "araucarioid" describes the bordered pits. The tracheids have a hexagonal, beehive-like outline and are alternately arranged in longitudinal rows. Today, this unique pit structure is found only in extant trees belonging to the *Araucaria* and *Agathis* genera. Specimens of petrified woods which exhibit these structures are known by various generic names: *Dadoxylon* (ill. 4.14), *Araucarioxlyon, Cordaitoxylon, Mesoxylon* and *Pennsylvanioxylon*. Secondary woods within these taxa are for the most part identical, but differences exist in the number of rows of bordered pits and in the heights of the usually single-rowed medullary rays. Except for the absence of annual rings and the presence of araucarioid pits, the woods of the various Cordaites are very similar in structure to the woods of modern coniferous trees. Although Cordaites flourished as extensive forests during the Carboniferous, the group seems to have become extinct during the Permian.

## Cladoxylales

Among the ferns (Pteridopsida), the extinct order Cladoxylales represents a unique evolutionary phase of the rather heterogeous Primofilices. Some Cladoxylales from the Middle Devonian to Lower Carboniferous periods show characteristics of primitive ferns. Transitional forms range from the primitive actinostele to various types of plectostele (*Cladoxylon scoparium, C. taeniatum*) (ill. 4.15), as well as vascular bundles of the eustele type (*Cladoxylon dubium*). In cross-section, individual vascular bundles appear to develop xylem (wood) in all directions, i.e., all around themselves. Opinions differ about this material: some experts believe it to be secondary xylem, others regard it merely as metaxylem. If one assumes that secondary xylem is indeed present, then this type of xylem distribution would strongly resemble that found in the Medullosaceae (seed fern) family, where (as in *Medullosa leuckartii*) each individual stele possesses its own round belt of secondary wood.

Ill. 4.15 Schematic cross-section of *Cladoxylon taeniatum*. The isolated vascular bundles produced secondary xylem toward all sides.

## Seed Ferns

Seed ferns (Pteridospermae) flourished in vast numbers and in many different varieties from the Carboniferous to the Lower Permian period. The external similarity between their shapes and those assumed by isospore ferns, as well as their reproduction by means of seeds, have sparked debates about the true identities of their closer and more distant relatives. Williamson (1872) was the first scientist to describe *Lyginodendron oldhamium* on the basis of a 1.6-inch (4-cm) thick specimen of seed-fern stem. A substantial pithy body is surrounded by five to nine vascular bundles. Secondary wood expands outward from the individual vascular bundles. Medullary (pith) rays form tapering wedges as they progress from the stem's interior to its periphery. Tracheids exhibit araucarioid pitting.

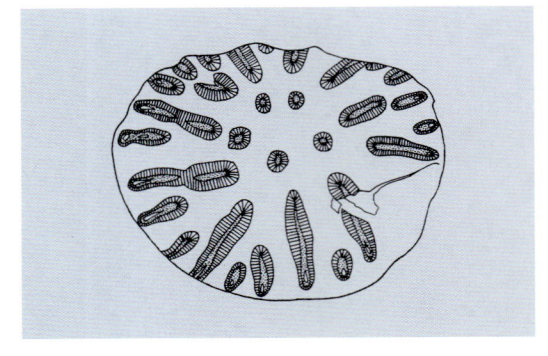

A second type of pteridosperm, known by the name *Medullosa*, belongs to the Medullosaceae family. Like the tree ferns, *Medullosa* trunks were surrounded by leaf-bases and roots. Depending on the arrangement of leaf traces, the interior of a *Medullosa* trunk may present a wide range of polystele variations, each composed of several isolated "meristeles." Meristeles (individual steles) tend to be more or less identical in older specimens

Secondary xylem; enlarged 26 times

Ill. 4.14 Permian *Dadoxylon*, Germany

Ill. 4.16 Permian *Medullosa*, Chemnitz

Ill. 4.17 Schematic cross-section of *Medullosa leuckartii*. The outer meristeles have grown into a nearly closed ring. Vascular bundles are each surrounded by secondary wood.

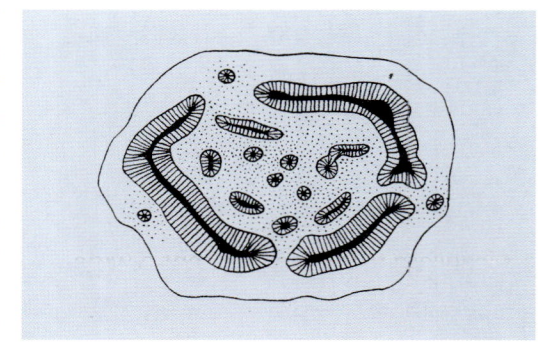

Ill. 4.18 *Medullosa*, showing star-shaped ring; enlarged 5 times

Ill. 4.19 Wood from a *Medullosa* with zone of primary xylem; enlarged 28 times

dating from the Carboniferous period, but more recent specimens of *Medullosa* from the Lower Permian (e.g., *Medullosa stellata* and its relatives) (ill. 4.16) exhibit a more complicated structure. In these specimens, small isolated meristeles occupy the center of the trunk. When viewed in cross-section, the outer meristeles seem to have fused together to form a nearly closed ring. Another characteristic feature of the *Medullosa* clan is readily seen when polished trunk slices are examined under a hand lens: within the steles, isolated or ring-shaped wood cells (i.e., secondary wood) are formed not only toward the periphery (centrifugal formation), but also toward the interior (centripetal formation) (ill. 4.19). Each individual stele (meristele) thus has its own round belt of secondary wood. Centripetal formation of secondary wood frequently creates distortions in the plant's tissue. Polysteles with secondary thickening toward all sides have become extinct; this type of growth has been interpreted as an unsuccessful adaptive strategy. This type of stele, together with its attribute of secondary thickening, can be regarded as a combination of characteristics common to both ferns and seed-bearing plants.

"Myeloxylon" describes petrified leaf stems from various species of *Medullosa*. Myeloxylon are distinguished by the presence of an atactostele. When viewed in cross-section, these specimens reveal a distribution of vascular bundles similar to that encountered among monocotyledenous plants, such as the various species of palms.

# Palm Ferns

The Mesozoic was the golden age of the palm ferns (Cycadopsida). These plants combine some characteristics common to the ferns (e.g., fronds) with other characteristics more commonly associated with seed-bearing plants (e.g., secondary wood and true seeds). Approximately 100 species in 9 different genera survive today. The important role played by the leaf-bases and the relatively small degree of wood formation (tracheids) are two features which the Cycadales share with the ferns. The stele construction (eustele) corresponds in principle to that found in the conifers and angiosperms. Broad medullary rays permeate the woody body as leaf holes. The wood of some cycads continues to show polyxyle structure in its secondary thickening. These are phylogenetic echoes of the belt-like thickening found around the polystele bundles of various types of *Medullosa* (seed ferns).

The Bennettitales (*Cycadeoidea*, ill. 4.20) were widely distributed during the Mesozoic era. Their knobby trunks were surrounded by an armor-like array of leaf-feet. These palm-fern-like gymnosperms (Bennettitopsida) had cauliform (stem-shaped) androgynous blossoms and are

Ill. 4.20 Jurassic *Cycadeoidea*, Utah

believed to have been pollinated by insects. Collectors frequently use the word "cycads" to describe slices of petrified Bennittales trunks. In cross-section and somewhat simplified, the trunk's anatomy is: a) typical eustele with considerable pith; b) protoxylem and secondary wood; c) massive bark with leaf-feet. A characteristic feature of the secondary wood are the transitions between netlike, laddered and bordered tracheids. Fossil specimens exhibiting this type of woody structure (*Paradoxoxylon, Sahnioxylon*) have been found in Japan, India, France, Switzerland, Germany and elsewhere.

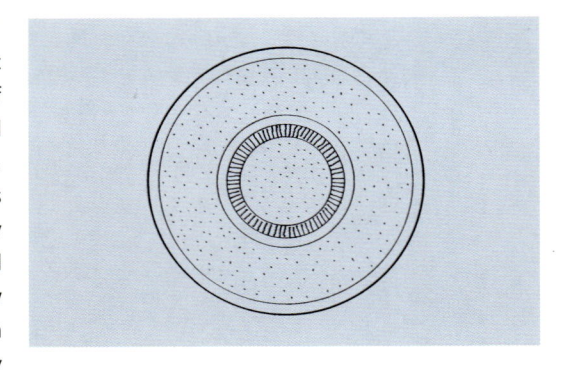

Ill. 4.21 Schematic cross-section of a cycadeoid stem. A large, central pith is surrounded by wood, followed by a narrow ring of phloem and relatively thick bark on the outer edge.

## Gymnosperms

The first true "woody trunks" appeared sometime during the Upper Devonian period, i.e., approximately 370 million years ago. This modern structural organization can be seen, for example, in trunks of *Archaeopteris-Callixylon*, a tree which grew to heights of up to 30 feet (9m) and reached diameters of as much as 5 feet (1.5m). These tree trunks developed massive secondary xylem, i.e., true wood composed of tracheids. The radially arranged cell walls of these tracheids (woody fibres) show araucarioid pitting. *Archaeopteris* thus combines certain fernlike characteristics (e.g., apparently feathery fronds and sporangia) with anatomical features (e.g., the woody trunk of *Callixylon*) present in today's extant gymnosperms.

## Needle-Bearing Trees

The wood of most gymnosperms is relatively simple in structure. Only two different types of "building block" cells - tracheids (woody fibres) and parenchyma cells - are present. The axially oriented longitudinal tracheid is the primordial form of the wood cell. When a trunk is cut in cross-section and polished, these axially oriented wood fibers are severed in transverse section. Under a hand lens, one can easily see the radially arranged rows of tracheids in the slice of petrified trunk. Between 90 and 94% of the wood from needle-bearing trees exhibits this monotonously structured woody body (pycnoxyle microstructure, ill. 4.23, 4.24). During the spring of the year, the vertically arranged, longitudinal tracheids are primarily involved in water transport; during the late summer, their principal function is to contribute to the tree's stability. During the spring, these cells are thin-walled and relatively large (wide-lumened) when viewed in cross-section; during the late summer, they form as thick-walled, radially flattened, narrow-lumened wood cells. These seasonal cycles create the concentric bordering lines (annual rings or growth zones) which are readily seen when a tree trunk is cut in cross-section. Parenchyma cells, which are usually somewhat darker in color, begin near the central pith and continue outward toward the bark. When viewed in cross-section, these medullary rays (pith rays or wood rays) interrupt the basic tissue and subdivide it into smaller segments. Under a hand lens, one can easily distinguish the medullary rays as radially running lines. Axially oriented tracheids cross the horizontally running medullary rays within the wood body. Where these two types of cells meet, they form rectangular radial wall planes, generally known as "fields of intersection." The wall structure of these fields of intersection (bordered pits) can only be seen under a microscope on thin sections under magnifications of 400 or more.

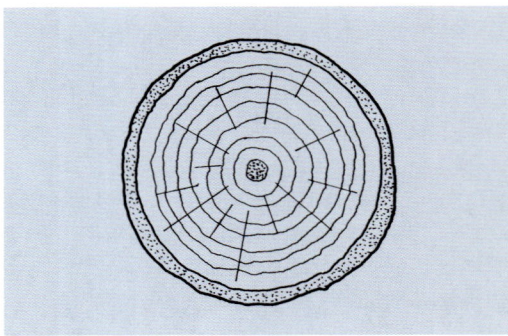

Ill. 4.22 Schematic cross-section of a woody stem. A small, central pith is surrounded by concentric growth zones and bark. The medullary rays run radially.

Ill. 4.23 Wood from a Tertiary needle-bearing tree, Oregon

Ill. 4.24 Wood with boundary of annual ring; enlarged 18 times

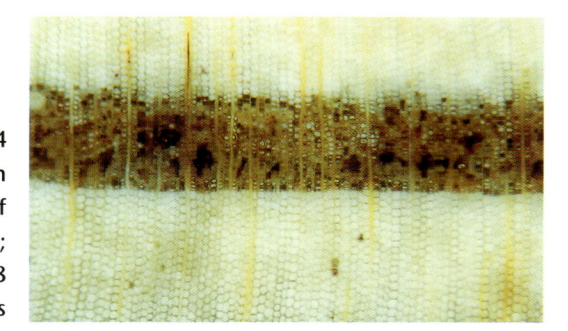

The arrangements and the types of structure exhibited by these field-of-intersection pits are decisive characteristics needed for positive identification of woods from needle-bearing trees. Without careful examination of the field-of-intersection pits, there can be no reliable identification of the species of needle-bearing tree from which a specimen of recent or petrified wood has come. If only a polished slice of trunk is available, precise botanical identification is simply not possible. Extant needle-bearing trees are assigned to 7 families comprising 49 genera and some 550 different species (Kubitzki 1990). Scientific journals in which petrified gymnosperms are anatomically described and identified have not yet been included within a comprehensive computerized database. (Data about petrified woods from decidous trees are available in computerized form.) Several hundred specialized journals have been published throughout the world.

## *Angiosperms, Deciduous Trees*

The "woody trunk" has become the dominant structural type among the needle-bearing and deciduous trees of our current geological era. This construction is apparently far superior to that which had been employed in all other, now-extinct types of trunks. Among trees indigenous to central Europe, the circumference of the self-enclosed, ring-shaped cambium increases by approximately 1000-fold. Gigantic exotic trees attain still higher values. Deciduous trees first appeared only about 100 million years ago during the hot, humid climate of the Middle Cretaceous period. In the course of some 25 million years (Barreme to Cenoman), the angiosperms (the "vessel-seeders" in constrast to the gymnosperms or "naked-seeders") came to dominate the world's vegetation. During the Cretaceous period (144 to 65 million years ago), the main groups of angiosperms established themselves in the holarctic, pantropical, and palaeotropical regions as well as in the southern hemisphere. At the end of the Cretaceous, on the threshold of the Tertiary, there existed an astonishing abundance of "vessel-seeders," especially angiosperms (flowering plants and deciduous trees). Angiosperms were particularly dominant in warmer, more nutrient-rich continental habitats. In the subsequent course of the Tertiary, this vegetation achieved an unprecedentedly high degree of diversity and differentiation. Associated with this was a parallel and almost explosive evolution in the animal world (insects, birds and mammals). Almost everywhere on the planet, the more ancient gymnosperms were driven back by the rapid advance of the dominant deciduous trees (angiosperms). The speedy

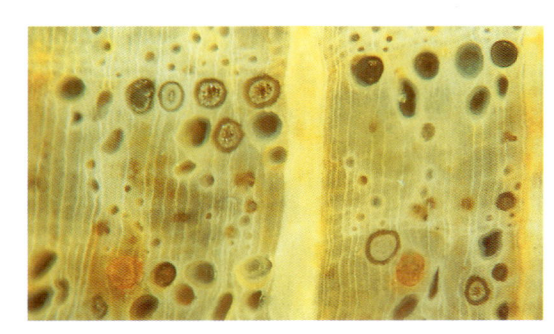

Ill. 4.25 Oak with ring-shaped pores; enlarged 18 times

Ill. 4.26 Tertiary oak; Oregon

Ill. 4.27 Tertiary maple, Oregon

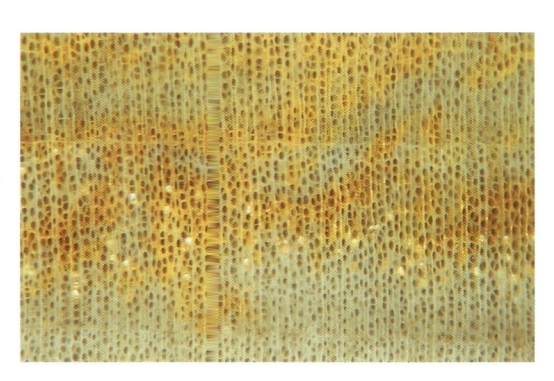

Ill. 4.28 Maple with scattered pores; enlarged 28 times

Ill. 4.30 Tangential section of Tertiary chestnut wood with two growth boundaries, Germany. Photo: A. Selmeier

global radiation of the angiosperms was encouraged by their evolution of blossoms, fruits and seeds which encouraged pollination and/or distribution by fauna. Gymnosperms persisted in building their wood according to the monotonous structural pattern of tracheid wood (pycnoxylic microstructure); but as early as the Tertiary, angiosperms had already evolved a never-before-seen diversity of wood anatomies. Angiosperm cambium produces a wide variety of highly diverse "building blocks." Approximately 163 different microscopic features should be considered when identifying angiosperm wood. This indicates that the division of labor within the woody tissue has progressed considerably compared to the monotony found in woods from needle-bearing trees. This increased diversity markedly improved the angiosperms' ability to adapt to a wide range of climates, zones of vegetation, and biotopes. Unlike the needle-bearing trees, angiosperms use specialized, axially oriented "tubes" for water transport. These conductive pathways (vessels, tracheids) appear in cross-section on polished trunk slices as "holes" or "pores" which are large enough to be seen with the naked eye. A magnifying glass often makes it possible for one's gaze to penetrate several millimeters into the three-dimensional structure of the woody tissue. Examining the pattern of distribution of these vessels in cross-section provides important data upon which to base an initial categorization.

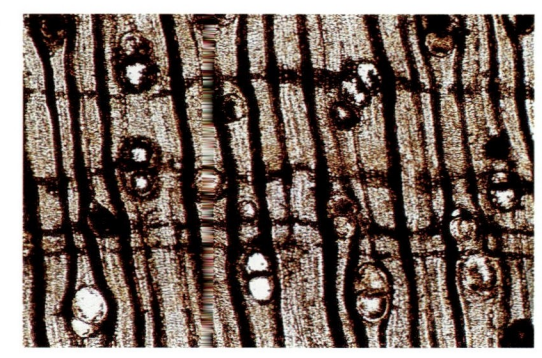

■ Angiosperm wood with a ring of pores: the large vessels of wood cells formed during the spring of the year lie immediately along the growth boundary; the diameter of the vessels becomes abruptly smaller as one progresses in a radial direction toward the next annual ring. Example: oak (Ill. 4.25, 4.26, 4.31). Approximately 6% of the most important recent angiosperms form wood with a ring of pores.

■ Angiosperm wood with scattered pores: vessels within one growth zone are all nearly equal in diameter and more or less equally distributed; there is no clearly discernible ring of pores. Example: maple (Ill. 4.27, 4.28). Approximately 90% of the most important recent angiosperms form wood with scattered pores. Certain angiosperm woods display transitional structures intermediate between those encountered in ring-of-pores woods and scattered-pore woods.

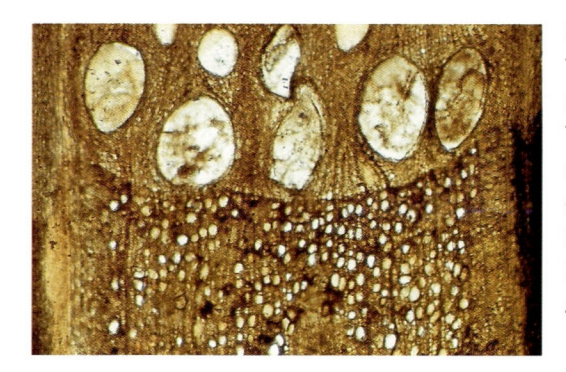

Ill. 4.29 Tertiary mahagony wood with four tangential bands of parenchyma, Germany. Photo: A. Selmeier

Ill. 4.31 Tangential section of Tertiary oak showing growth boundary. Photo: A. Selmeier

Please note: Without thin sections or thin slides cut and polished along all three axes (transverse, radial and tangential), it is impossible to reliably identify recent or fossil specimens of wood from deciduous trees. The number of living species of angiosperms is estimated at about 25,000, distributed among 342 families. Adequate research into their technical and anatomical attributes has been conducted only on the approximately 3,000 varieties of wood commonly available on commercial markets. Petrified angiosperm woods have been described, discussed according to 163 distinguishing characteristics, and identified in more than 1,000 scientific publications. These publications have been organized in a computerized database.

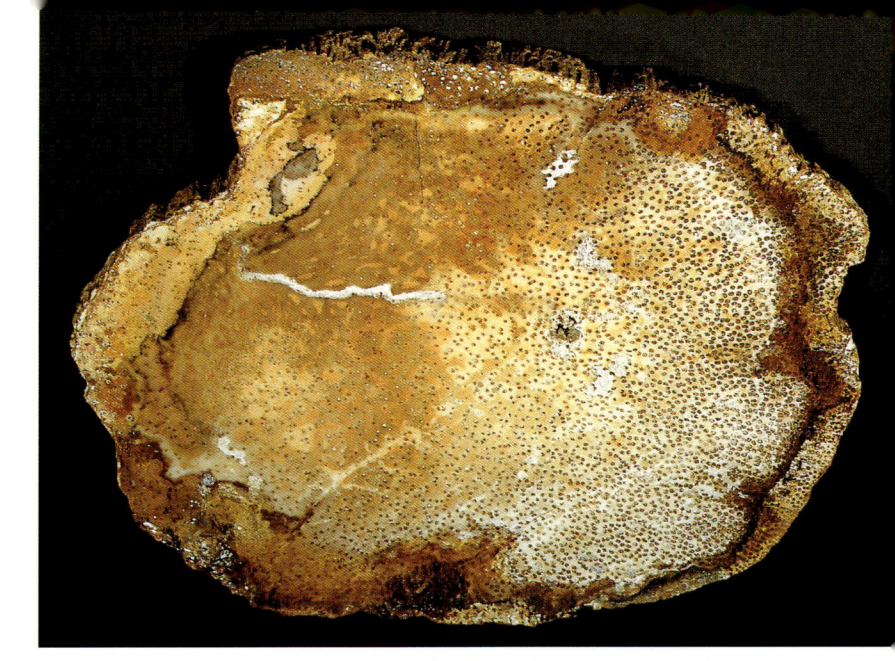

Ill. 4.33 Tertiary palm, Louisiana

## Monocotyledenous Woods

Sytematic botany divides the seed-bearing plants into gymnosperms, monocotyledons (one cotyledon at the beginning of growth) and dicotyledons (two cotyledons). Thanks to their secondary thickening ("wood" production), gymnosperms and dicotyledenous woody plants are able to increase the girth of their stems. Among the monocotyledons, on the other hand, there are only a few "true" woody plants. Some examples are the *Aloe, Cordyline, Dracaena,* and *Yucca* genera. Throughout the course of evolution, these genera have remained as isolated special cases among the monocotyledonous plants. Their secondary thickening proceeds in a different fashion than seen in gymnosperms and deciduous trees. A well-known example of abnormal secondary growth in girth is seen among the dragon trees (*Dracaena draco*) on the Canary Islands.

Ill. 4.32 Vascular bundles in basic tissue of Tertiary palm wood, Louisiana

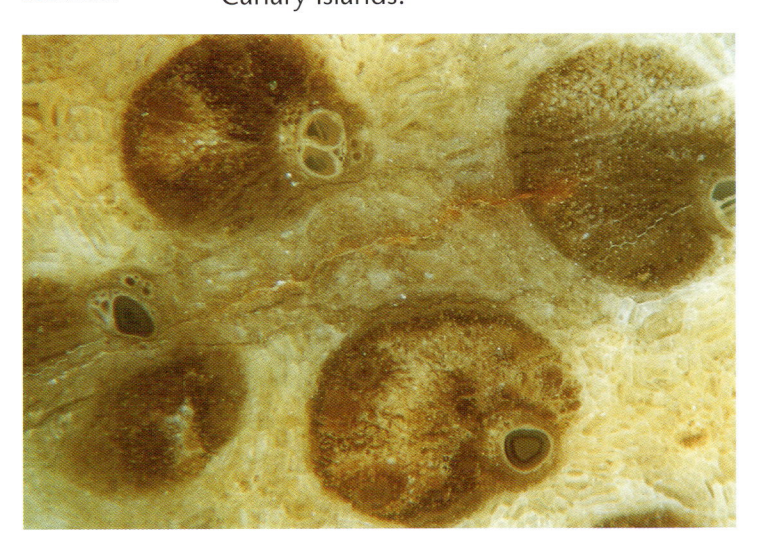

## Palms

Among the palms, cell production at the sprout tip leads to growth not only in length, but also in girth. Unlike the needle-bearing and broad-leaved trees, palms do not develop a ring-shaped cambium which cyclically releases xylem (wood) cells toward the tree's center in a seasonal rhythm, nor do they exhibit secondary thickening. Although the name palm "wood" is commonly used, the appellation is anatomically incorrect. Collateral vascular bundles with diameters ranging from 0.5 to 1.5 millimeters are distributed across the entire surface of the transverse section (ill. 4.32, 4.33). Isolated from one another, these bundles lie within a loosely structured basic tissue made of parenchyma. On polished trunk slices, the numerous, widely strewn, mostly brownish vascular bundles appear as fairly large "dots." Solutions of monomolecular silicic acid easily penetrate the loosely structured basic tissue; vascular bundles, on the other hand, are relatively resistant to penetration by silicic acid solutions. Because they resist penetration by silicic acids, they are often subject to decomposition and are less likely to be well preserved. Differences in permeability thus create numerous "holes" or "tubes." This so-called "canaliculatus structure" is readily seen with the naked eye and serves as a typical distinguishing feature of petrified palm "woods." Other fossilized woods that have been bored by *Teredo* (ship-worms) or termites should not be confused with specimens exhibiting the true canaliculatus structure found in petrified palm trunks.

# Tree Ferns - Past and Present

Rafael Herbst

Ill. 5.1 Tree ferns in the Brazilian jungle; photo: H. Klein

Ill. 5.1a Cross-section of a recent tree fern, Brazil; photo: H. Klein

Ill. 5.2 *Psaronius sp.*, Hilbersdorf, Germany

Ill. 5.3 Excerpt showing aerial root, enlarged 30 times

In this article I'd like to discuss petrified tree ferns. "Forests" of this kind are far less commonly known than petrified forests featuring the trunks of conifers or angiosperm trees. The reasons for this are twofold: first, even in the past, tree ferns were never very common; secondly, their trunks would seem to have been less amenable to fossilization. In most cases, tree ferns never formed monocultural forests of tree ferns alone, but grew instead as lower-growing plants beneath the canopy of the taller trees (ill. 5.1, 5.1a). They preferred to grow in warm and moist regions, especially along the shores of rivers and lakes. These preferences

Ill. 5.4 *Tietea singularis,* Brazil

thus restricted them to a limited range of habitats. Fossil tree ferns have been found in large numbers at a few sites, so that it has become possible to reconstruct the probable appearance of an ancient tree fern. Petrified trunks serve as the basis for these reconstructions; artists' renderings have been published in a great many textbooks and other publications. Along with the trunks of these tree ferns, the same or adjacent sediments have also yielded fossils of fronds from the same tree ferns (ill. 3.2).

Well-preserved stems have been recovered from two groups of ferns. On the one hand, there is the order Marattiales, which comprises the dominant group of Upper Palaeozoic ferns. Relatives of these ferns still grow today, for example in the so-called "*Macroangiopteris* forests" of Australia. The second major group includes the Osmundales, which first appeared as primitive forms during the Permian period and then went on to colonize much of the planet during the Mesozoic. Today, only three genera of non-arboreal habit are still extant.

Ill. 5.5 *Tuvichapteris solmsi,* Paraguay

Ill. 5.6 Excerpt showing egress of the petiole

Ill. 5.7 *Psaronius infarctus*, Hilbersdorf, Germany

## Marattiaces

The Marattiales (ill. 5.2, 5.3) represent an ancient group of rather primitive ferns that had primitively structured sporangia called "synangia." They attained tree size and habit early in the plant kingdom's evolutionary line. They reached these heights by evolving progressively more complex arrangements of what was originally a simple structure comprising a very few meristeles. Meristeles contain mostly xylem; they are surrounded by parenchyma and strengthened with schlerenchymatic fibers. Two types of meristeles appeared: the so-called caulinar strands which, while traversing upward, radiate petiolar strands that in turn leave the stem to become the vascular bundles for the large fronds.

Ill. 5.8 *Psaronius sp.*, Ohio USA

Ill. 5.9
*Guairea carnieri*, Paraguay

Although the trunks of these Marattiales resemble inverted cones, i.e., have a smaller diameter at their bases than at their tops, the trunk nevertheless looks like the trunk of a "normal" tree - thicker below, more slender above. The reason for this lies in the characteristically massive root mantle which is composed of hundreds or thousands of individual roots.

Ill. 5.10  Excerpt from the central cylinder

Ill. 5.11  *Millerocaulis sp.*, Tasmania, Australia; photo and collection: R. Hewer

152

Ill. 5.12 Petiole of *Osmundacaulis sp.*, enlarged 40 times, Tasmania, Australia

## Three Genera

At least three Marattiace genera are known. *Psaronius* is mainly found in the northern hemisphere; *Tietiea* (ill. 5.4) and *Tuvichapteris* (ill. 5.5, 5.6) have only been collected in South America to date. Specimens of the former have been known as *"Starsteine"* ("starling-stone") for centuries; they have often been used as gemstones in jewelry, and can be admired in many European museums. Especially the roots of these petrifications display magnificent and widely varied colors.

Ill. 5.13 Excerpt of *Osmundacaulis sp.*, showing central cylinder and xylem, enlarged 13 times, Tasmania, Australia

Ill. 5.14 *Osmundacaulis sp.*, Tasmania, Australia

The leaves of *Psaronius* seem to have been quite varied and have been assigned to several different genera including *Asterotheca*, *Acitheca*, *Scolecopteris* and many others.

The region surrounding Chemnitz, Germany (5.7) has yielded so many *Psaronius* stems that it deserves to be regarded as a true petrified forest. Most discoveries occurred during the 19th and early 20th centuries. Additional discovery sites are located in Nová Paka, Czech Republic and in Austin, France, as well as in the United States, where coal balls have been found in Ohio and elsewhere. Fern stems and other remains (ill. 5.8) account for as much as 30% of the petrifications at these sites.

# Osmundales

The other interesting group of ferns which attained tree size is the Osmundales. The genus *Osmunda* is the best-known extant representative of this group, although no modern *Osmunda* grows to tree-like heights. There is much diversity in the structure of Osmundales trunks, but they are essentially composed of a xylematic central cylinder with a relatively small pith surrounded by a number of individual meristeles that radiate from this cylinder. The meristeles run obliquely upward, emerging as petioles in the fronds. The most common ones associated with these plants have been named *Cladophlebis* and have a very general fern morphology that does not differ from that of many extant ferns.

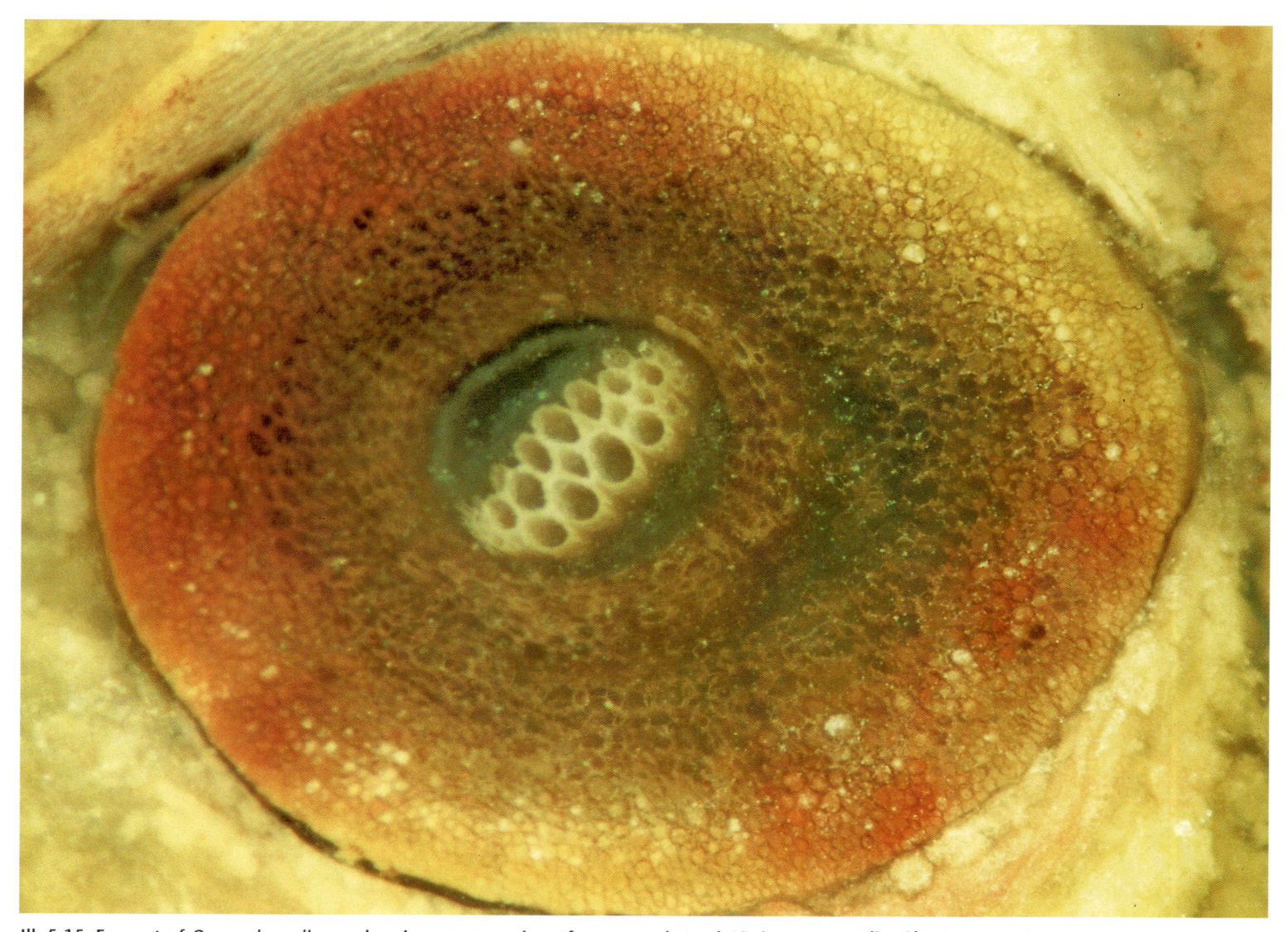

Ill. 5.15 Excerpt of *Osmundacaulis sp.*, showing cross-section of a root, enlarged 40 times, Australia, Slg. Norman Donpon

Well-preserved petrified Permian stems from Australia have been described as *Paleosmunda*; *Guairea* (ill. 5.9, 5.10) is the representative of a mainly South American family of Osmundales. These plants, which represent an early phylogenetic phase, nevertheless possess a highly complex anatomical structure.

The best-preserved and most widely distributed genera *Osmundacaulis* (ill. 5.12, 5.13, 5.14, 5.15, 5.16) and *Millerocaulis* (ill. 5.11) flourished throughout virtually the entire Mesozoic. Beautiful examples of Osmundalian forests are found in Australia in the Lune River area of Tasmania and at Miles, Queensland. Another noteworthy site is at Gran Bajo de San Julian in Patagonia, Argentina.

They are frequently found together with marvelously well-preserved wood from the trunks of araucarioid trees.

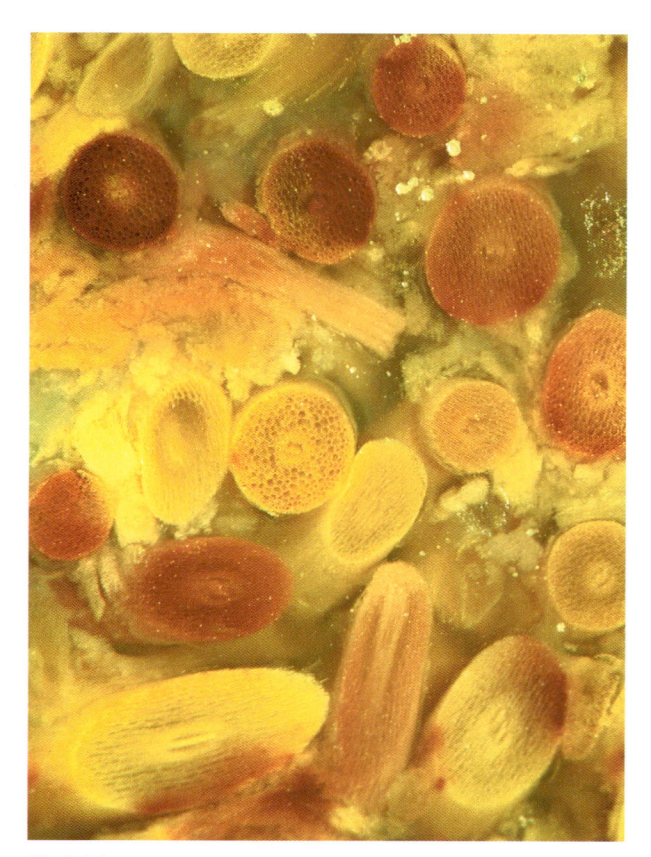

Ill. 5.16
Excerpt showing roots of *Osmundacaulis sp.*, enlarged 22 times, Australia, Slg. Norman Donpon

Ill. 6.1 Leaf of a later, seed-fern variety of Lower Jurassic *Sagenopteris rhoifolia*, Germany, State Collection, Munich. Photo: F. Höck

# Ferns, Cycads, or What?

## Walter Jung

Adolphe Brongniart, who is widely regarded as one of the fathers of palaeobotany, published in 1828 a number of different names for fern-like Palaeozoic fronds in his monumental and never-completed work *Histoire des Végétaux Fossiles*. All of these names bore the suffix *-pteris*, the Greek word for "fern." Since other scientists of Brongiart's generation repeatedly asserted that the late Palaeozoic era was extraordinarily rich in fern varieties, this division of the Earth's history was soon popularly referred to as "The Age of Ferns." Doubts, however, gradually arose about the ferny nature of the by no means uncommon fossil fronds. Although palaeobotanists continued to classify them within the fern clan, most fronds lacked the heap-like clusters of sporangia (sori) that distinguish true ferns. Dionys Stur therefore postulated that they might in fact belong to a heretofore unknown group of plants. This suggestion received further corroboration in 1887, when Williamson announced that the anatomy of some fossil trunks justified placing them in a category of their own, intermediate between ferns and cycads. A few years later, in 1899, Potenié Sr. grouped these plants under the name Cycadofilices. This stroke of genius was soon followed by a startling discovery: English palaeobotanists Oliver and Scott announced in 1904 that the "fern" fronds known to Brongniart as *Sphenopteris hoeninghausi* actually bore true seeds and that they in fact belonged to the already well-known *Dadoxylon oldhamium* clan within the new Cycadofilices group. Oliver and Scott coined the name "pteridosperms" ("seed ferns") to describe these plants. The appellation gained popularity in ensuing years, and subsequently discovered fossils swelled the ranks of the pteridosperms as many newly unearthed specimens were placed within this group.

The correct German word for pteridosperm is *Farnsamer*, although in some literature they are mistakenly called *Samenfarne*. Their discovery has frequently been hailed as "the greatest contribution that fossil botany has made to our knowledge of evolution in the plant kingdom." For fairness' sake, however, we ought to mention that at almost the same time, Grand'Eury found through his examination of French fossil material that some of the so-called "fern" fronds bore seeds, and went on to conclude that the plants which bore those fronds must therefore have been "primitive cycads."

The origins of the pteridosperms can be traced to the Upper Devonian period. Their more remote ancestors lie still further back, and should probably be sought among the progymnosperms of the Middle Devonian. After enjoying their first focus of development during the Late Palaeozoic era, several highly evolved groups again flourished during the Middle Mesozoic era (ill. 6.1, 6.3). The seed ferns finally died out during the Lower Cretaceous period; their demise coincided with the rise of the angiosperms.

Ill. 6.3 Leaf of a later, seed-fern form of Upper Triassic *Dicroidium odontopteroides*, South Africa, State Collection, Munich. Photo: F. Höck

Ill. 6.2 Frond from an Upper Carboniferous *Neuropteris ovata*, Germany, State Collection, Munich. Photo: F. Höck

## *Medullosa* – Rich in Pith

Among the various Palaeozoic pteridosperms, the members of the genus *Medullosa* deserve our special attention. Just as in the animal kingdom, where there is a certain degree of justification for referring to birds as "the last dinosaurs," so too in the plant kingdom it is not entirely exaggerated to regard extant cycads as the last surviving seed ferns.

Ill. 6.4 Polished section of trunk from a Lower Permian *Medullosa stellata*, Germany, State Collection, Munich. Photo: F. Höck

Both the faunal and flora examples are admittedly somewhat provocative, but they help to emphasize undeniably close phylogenetic links.

A statement of this sort is only possible because so much is known about the morphological and anatomical details of the Medullosaceae. The frequently encountered assertion that this ancient plant family is practically as well known as other, extant groups is, in fact, only mildly overstated.

Along with the fronds (primarily of the *Neuropteris* and *Alethopteris* types), the pollen blossoms (e.g., *Whittleseya, Dolerotheca* and *Aulacotheca*), and the up-to-10-centimeter-large seeds of especially the genera *Trigonocarpus* (casts) (ill. 6.5) and *Pachytesta* (permineralizations), it is above all the *Medullosa* trunks with their marvelously well-preserved structural features that help to justify this assertion. These ancient trunks measure up to 26.4 feet (8 m) in length and as much as 19.6 inches (50 cm) in diameter. Polished cross-sections of *Medullosa* trunks typically display two or more vascular bundles embedded in the "pith," with each bundle surrounded by a ring of secondary wood. This unusual and in the plant kingdom nearly unique type of interior trunk construction has been described, especially in older literature, as "polystele" (many-bundled). More recent research has shown that the number of vascular bundles varies with the evolutionary level of the plant and that the several vascular bundles can be traced back to a single, deeply divided bundle. Fossils of such trunks are still sometimes surrounded by their massive frond basis (*Myeloxylon*).

In geologically more recent varieties (such as the Lower Permian *Medullosa stellata*, ill. 6.4), the peripheral vascular bundles have fused to create one or more rings displaying an inner (centripetal) and an outer (centrifugal) layer of secondary wood. Numerous and very tiny individual bundles, embedded within the basic tissue, are found at the inmost center of the trunk. Astonishingly well-preserved fossils of this sort have been discovered in the petrified forest at Chemnitz and in the gravel beds at Autun in central France. Bernhard Cotta, who coined the name *"Medullosa"* in 1832, did so on the basis of specimens unearthed at Chemnitz.

## Trees and Lianas

Along with this diversity in their trunk anatomy, *Medullosas* also showed heterogeneity in their growth habits. In addition to the already mentioned, several-meter-tall, tree-like varieties with outer layers of bark, root-mantles at the bases of their trunks, and long-lasting "leaf bases" (all of these details are visible in most reconstructions), the *Medullosa* clan also seems to have included lianas and climbing vines whose slender trunks, which seldom measured more than a few centimeters in diameter, were probably unable to stand erect on their own. As mentioned earlier, many different types of fronds have been discovered: some examples include the "organ genera" *Neuropteris* (ill.6.2) *Alethopteris, Odontopteris, Linopteris, Lonchopteris* and *Eusphenopteris*. Variations also existed in the size of the seeds, which ranged from veritable giants down to dwarfs measuring only a few millimeters in diameter. Pollen grains, on the other hand, were extraordinarily large; some of them attained stately dimensions in excess of 0.5 millimeter. Their large sizes and the discovery of this type of pollen on the feet of the gigantic *Arthropleura* millipede suggest that some or perhaps all *Medullosa* pollen grains were transferred from one plant to the next by animals.

Two final points remain to be made. First, it is remarkable that, among today's gymnosperms, only the cycads still produce fern-like leaf fronds; female *Cycas* specimens even bear fern-like seed fronds (megasporophylls). Second, it is likewise noteworthy that the rise of the Cycadophytes more or less coincided with the demise of the *Medullosas*. Although many similarities exist between these two groups (which limitations of space prevent us from examining in greater detail here), the two groups ought not to be conjoined. Their differences are too obvious to justify such a conflation. One need only consider the heterogeneity in the design of their male flowering organs: *Medullosas* produce complexly built, sometimes cup-shaped or disk-shaped structures whose arrangement can be traced back to a still frond-like fundamental model; cycads, on the other hand, bear massive floral cones composed of numerous, scale-shaped microsporophylls.

In any case, and as far as current palaeobotanical knowledge extends, we can certainly conclude that the pteridosperms as a whole are one of the best-known groups of fossil plants and that their investigation has yielded a wealth of new insights into the lives of prehistoric plants.

Ill. 6.5
Cast of a seed from an Upper Carboniferous *Trigonocarpus noeggerathii*, Czech Republic, State Collection, Munich.
Photo: F. Höck

# Cycadophytes - Plant Relics from the Days of the Dinosaurs

**Friedemann Schaarschmidt**

Ill. 7.3
*Macrozamia sp.*
Fraser Island, Queensland, Australia

# A Silicified Trunk in Baroque Dresden

Ill. 7.1 *Cycadeoidea ("Raumeria") reichenbachiana*, Cretaceous silicified trunk with numerous flower buds between its leaf bases, found in Silesia in 1753, length ca. 1.6 feet (0.5 m), Wieliczka, Poland, Dresden Museum, photo: B. Bastian.

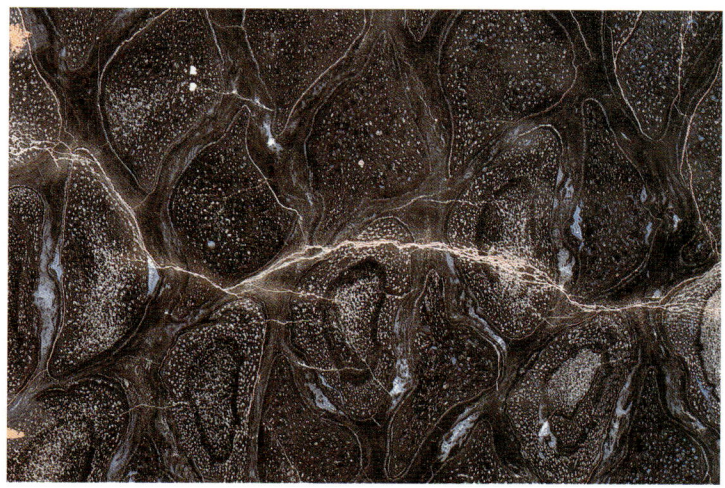

Ill. 7.2 *Cycadeoidea ("Raumeria") reichenbachiana*, longitudinal section through the region of leaf bases; this thin section was prepared by Wieland from the Dresden specimen shown in Ill. 7.1.

Archduke Friedrich August of Saxony, known as "August the Strong," ascended the Polish throne in 1797, reigning there as King August II. In accord with the spirit of that era, he sought to imitate in Saxony the style of court life practiced in France by "Sun King" Louis XIV. Extending royal patronage to a variety of cultural activities - including art collections and natural history collections - was an important part of that courtly style. Dresden's gallery of paintings, for example, and its famous "Green Vault" are deeply indebted to August's patronage. Natural history collections also enjoyed a period of rapid growth during this era. These collections began in 1587 and had their roots in Saxony's thriving mining industry, an activity that naturally brought to light and encouraged the collection of unusual minerals and rare fossils. It is therefore not surprising to learn that it was a Saxon named Georg Agricola who wrote the first basic book about the techniques of mining. August the Strong's son, who became Poland's King August III, continued to support his father's cultural ambitions. It is to his credit that Dresden's geological collections at the State Museum for Mineralogy and Geology now number among the oldest and most significant in Germany.

Ill. 7.4 Jurassic *Cycadeoidea sp.* from Utah, longitudinal section of trunk in the region of the leaf bases; iron oxide has colored this specimen red.

Ill. 7.6 Cretaceous *Cycadeoidea sp.*, a group of three from South Dakota, Senckenberg Museum of Natural History; photo: S. Tränker.

Ill. 7.7 *Cycadeoidea sp.*, surface of the trunk with a bud; excerpt from specimen shown in Ill. 7.6.

One particularly unusual fossil can be found in that collection. This specimen is of extraordinarily great value to science, and it is associated with an interesting story. During the mid-18th century, whenever a rare mineral or fossil specimen was unearthed anywhere in the Saxony or Poland, it would usually be sent to Dresden. And this is precisely what happened in 1753, when Borlach sent to August III's "Cabinet of Natural Curiosities" in Dresden a silicified tree stump that had been found two years earlier in a swamp near Lednica, not far from the salt mines at Wieliczka, Poland. The trunk (ill. 7.1, 7.2) survived all subsequent events in Dresden, including the Zwinger Fire of 1849 (which it survived unscathed within a sandstone column) and the catastrophic air raid of February 13, 1945. This silicified specimen is 1.6 feet (0.5 m) long and equally wide; it weighs some 450 pounds (200 kg); and it no doubt evoked widespread astonishment when it was first discovered. Today, the specimen still draws admiring gazes in the museum, although it represents only one intermediate segment of an original trunk which might well have measured some 3.3 feet (1 m) in length. The specimen has almost always been regarded as a plant fossil, although shortly after its discovery, Eilenburg suggested that it might represent the remains of ancient coral. Its superficial appearance suggested that it could be the "crown of a petrified palm." In his *Natural History of Petrifications* (1773), Prof. of Rhetoric J.E.I. Walch agreed with this opinion about the fossil's identity. It is to be expected that these interpretations, because they date from the "prescientific era" of palaeobotany, are liable to be less than entirely accurate. Nearly a century would pass before Heinrich Robert Göppert, the "father of German palaeobotany," would publish the first scientific treatment of this fossil in 1853. He named it *"Raumeria reichenbachiana"* and classed it among the cycads. His classification was not entirely mistaken.

# Cycads - Peculiar Gymnosperms

But what exactly is a "cycad"? In our latitudes, members of this plant family thrive only in greenhouses. A few can be bought in flower shops, and *Cycas revoluta* is sometimes even sold in supermarkets as a houseplant. Some readers may even own (and regularly water) one of them without realizing just how remarkable this organism actually is.

Because the cycads are not endemic to modern Germany, there was no German name for the plant. Several names were proposed, but none of them proved itself especially convincing. We shall therefore continue to use the scientific appellations "*Cycas*" and "cycads."

The overwhelming majority of today's plants are flowering plants or angiosperms. These plants all enclose their seeds in an ovary which later ripens to become a berry, nut or drupe. Cycads, on the other hand, are gymnosperms ("naked-seeders"). Other members of the gymnosperm group include familiar needle-bearing trees (conifers) like the pines, firs and spruces, as well as trees in the ginkgo group like the more or less familiar *Ginkgo biloba* (cf. p. 176 ff.) Gymnosperm seeds may be borne unprotected at the ends of stalks (like those produced by the ginkgo) or else they may form on the upper side of cone scales (as seen among the conifers). Primordial cycads formed their seeds along the edges of specially adapted leaves; in other genera, these leaves later grouped together to form cones.

Of the various kinds of gymnosperms, only the conifers are still widely distributed today. In cool temperate regions of the Northern Hemisphere, they form a "coniferous belt" of unbroken forest that spans the globe from Canada, across northern Europe and eastern Asia, and into the taiga of Siberia. The Siberian taiga extends especially far southwards because of the prevailing continental climate.

Although in the past the ginkgo order enjoyed wide distribution, the ginkgo very nearly became extinct in the wild, surviving only as a relic population confined to a very limited area in China. Like the ginkgo, today's cycads are also relics of a once widely developed and broadly distributed gymnosperm group that has existed for some 240 million years. Flourishing especially during the Mesozoic, these ancient plants shared the planet with the dinosaurs. Today, only about 160 species of cycads in 11 genera still survive; these survivors grow in isolated populations throughout the tropics and subtropics. These living cycads seem to be the last descendants of the *Medullosas*, a group of ancient plants which is classed among the seed ferns (see "Ferns, Cycads, or What?").

Today's surviving cycad genera grow in a variety of shapes. Some of them have a trunk crowned by a crest of pinnate leaves and look much like palm trees. Others, such as *Macrozamia* (ill. 7.3), have a very short trunk so that their crown of leaves seems to emerge directly from the ground. Cycad leaves can be simple (as they are in *Cycas*); some species have doubly pinnate leaves; in a few kinds, the pinnae have developed into protective thorns (*Encephalartos horridus*, for example). Cycad seeds form on the edges of stunted leaves whose upper portions may still show remnants of the leaf's original pinnate structure. The seeds of other cycad genera grow in cones which, like those borne by *Encephalartos*, may weigh as much as 218 pounds (45 kg).

Ill. 7.8 Upper Cretaceous *Monanthesia magnifica* from New Mexico, trunk with leaf bases and flower buds, State Collection, Munich; photo: F. Höck.

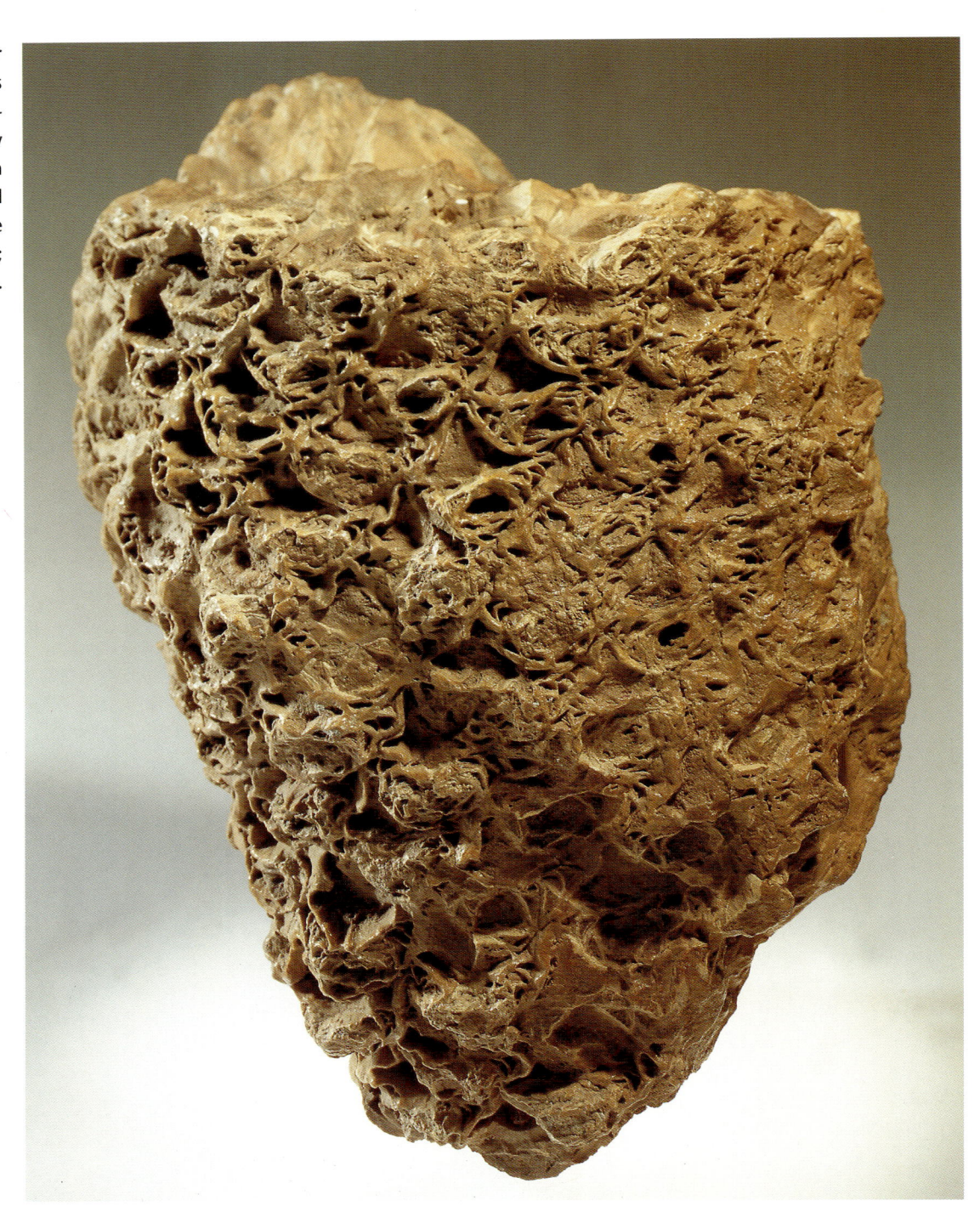

## The Bennettites - Dinosaurs of the Plant Kingdom

When Göppert classed *Raumeria reichenbachiana* among the cycads in 1853, he had undoubtedly found the group of living plants which is most closely related to this peculiar fossil. As early as the 19th century, botanists had correctly realized that the extant cycads are indeed very ancient plants. We know today that cycads enjoyed their greatest flourishing during the Mesozoic. Fossil remains of pinnate leaves which surely belonged to cycad plants are not uncommon. Particularly important are the numerous fossils in which we can discern seed-bearing leaves like those borne by *Cycas*. These leaves still retain the pinnate form and two-rowed arrangement of seeds typical of modern *Cycas*. Fossils of this sort have been found in Lower Permian strata in Europe, North America and China. Silicified trunks have been discovered in Triassic or Jurassic strata from Antarctica, North America, Argentina and India. It is now known that the trunks of Mesozoic and more recent cycads were relatively thin and slender, and that the modern tuberous trunks did not appear until the Tertiary. However, tuberous trunks of the "*Raumeria*" type are frequently found in Mesozoic strata, especially in Upper Jurassic and Lower Cretaceous fossils. Even prior to Göppert's 1853 publication, many similar discoveries had also been reported in Europe, for example from the Isle of Portland and the Isle of Wight. Although Göppert compared his own *Raumeria* with Buckland's description of *Cycadeoidea microphylla*, he did not entirely recognize the full extent of the correspondences between these two genera.

Nevertheless, his publication attracted the attention of the world's palaeobotanists to the Dresden specimen. A large number of tuberous trunks of the genus *Cycadeoidea* were subsequently unearthed in North America during the second half of the 19th century. Discovered at sites in Maryland, Wyoming, Kansas, Colorado, California, Texas and New Mexico, the most gorgeously colored trunks are no doubt those found in Utah (ill. 7.4).

The Black Hills of South Dakota are famous for the abundance of "cycads" found there. This relatively small but nonetheless striking mountain massif rises above the flat lands of the Great Plains east of the main massif of the Rocky Mountains. The Black Hills' granite center is surrounded by more recent sediments, especially Jurassic and Lower Cretaceous deposits. Early in the 19th century, Wilson P. Hunt's expedition found petrified woods in these sediments; some expedition members collected a few of these petrifications for use as whetstones. Shortly before the turn of the century, Lester F. Ward collected a large number of such specimens and published his findings. Subsequent research was performed by G.R. Wieland at Yale University in New Haven, Connecticut. With its collection of more than 1,000 trunks, Yale's Peabody Museum houses the world's largest collection of "cycads." None of these trunks are true cycads, but are instead "Bennittitales" or, to use a name common in North America, "Cycadeoidales."

Some Bennettites bear a certain superficial resemblance to cycads; the former have been extinct since the Upper Cretaceous, but would seem to have played a more important role than the cycads during the Mesozoic. Both groups are sometimes subsumed under the more inclusive term "*Cycadophytes.*"

Petrified *Cycadeoidea* trunks represent the geohistorical climax and the denouement of the Bennettites. Dying out during the course of the Cretaceous, their extinction coincided with the rise of the angiosperms and the demise of the dinosaurs. Although only a relatively few *Cycadeoidea* fossils have been unearthed outside of North America, petrified trunks have occasionally been found at sites throughout the world (e.g., Mexico, Italy, France, Belgium, England, Austria, Poland, Germany, India and Patagonia - ill. 7.5). These discoveries suggest that the genera must have enjoyed nearly worldwide distribution. Representative specimens from the Black Hills have since found their way into museums around the world. A few years ago, Frankfurt's Senckenberg Museum of Natural History acquired a lovely three-part grouping of South Dakotan provenance (ill. 7.6, 7.7). *Monanthesia*, a close relative of *Cycadeoidea*, forms all of its blossoms at the same time. A specimen of *Monanthesia magnifica*, originally discovered by Navajo Indians, then given by Hirmer to Wieland during the 1920s, is currently on display in the Bavarian State Collection in Munich (ill. 7.8).

Ill. 7.9
Reconstruction of *Cycadeoidea sp.* after Delevoryas (1971).

## Bennettites - Precursors of Our Flowering Plants?

The Bennettites evolved a wide variety of growth forms, but they all share a common reproductive anatomy. The ovaries and stamens are grouped closely together in conelike or blossomlike organs. In many genera, and for the first time in the history of the plant kingdom, these reproductive structures are hermaphroditic, containing both female and male organs. Standing upon a central axis, the stalked ovaries are covered with sterile seed-scales; above the seeds, these scales fuse to form a solid, armor-like structure pierced only by tiny holes. The stamens, which frequently contain a large number of pollen sacs, are arranged in a

Ill. 7.10 Construction of a *Cycadeoidea sp.* blossom with fully developed stamens; the conical female "cone" in the center does not begin to develop until after the stamens have withered; after Crepet (1974).

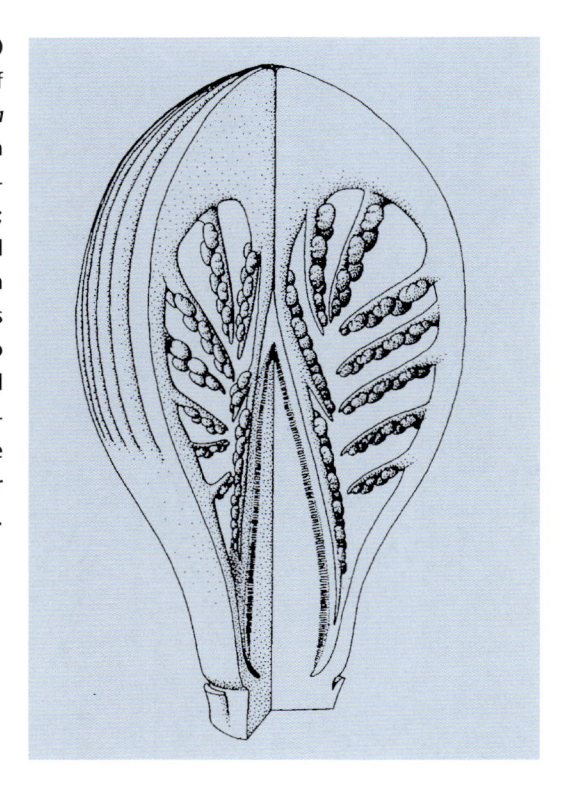

circle around the ovary. This circular arrangement is similar to that commonly seen in flowering plants. The size and construction of these sexual organs vary widely from one genus to another. The Bennettites' attempt to enclose their seeds led earlier botanists to regard them as ancestors of the angiosperms. But just as the cones of coniferous plants do not represent direct predecessors of angiosperm flowers, so too the Bennittites' flowers are not, in fact, precursors of true angiosperm blossoms. Apparent similarities are the result of parallel but unrelated evolutionary developments.

The presence of hermaphroditic flowers in both groups led early researchers to wonder whether Bennettite blossoms had perhaps been pollinated by insects. Current evidence suggests that Upper Carboniferous fauna may have helped transfer the male microspores of certain Bennettite ancestors. At first, this assistance may have happened more or less accidentally while the animals were feeding on parts of the blossoms, since protein-rich pollen is a much sought after food. The pollen of *Encephalartos*, a genus of African cycad, is still transferred by beetles today.

Scientists hoped that the abundant and often well-preserved *Cycadeoidea* fossils might shed light on the highly interesting question of the coevolutionary relationships between plants and insects. The tuberous trunks (ill. 7.9) of *Cycadeoidea* are densely covered with leaf bases and chaffy scales. One usually finds a large number of blossoms in the interstices between these scaly structures. Wieland and others had long believed that these blossoms, like those borne by our modern deciduous plants, would have opened their petals to attract insects. Unfortunately, the question of insect pollination could not be answered for this important genus. Throughout his many years of work at Yale University, T. Delevoryas consistently observed that the blossoms were always closed and that many of these flowers were fossilized or petrified in variously advanced stages of decay. These observations led him to conclude that they never actually opened and were very likely self-fertilizing. Crepet later discovered feeding tunnels which insects had delved into such blossoms. Current palaeobotanical opinion agrees that *Cycadeoidea* were largely self-fertilizing, but admits the possibility that voracious insects such as beetles may have played some role in the pollination process (ill. 7.10).

This function seems uniquely confined to the blossoms of *Cycadeoidea*. It surely did not occur among other Bennettites like *Williamsonia*, whose growth form superficially resembles the palms and from which a large number of calyx-shaped, open, unisexual blossoms have been found; nor has it been documented among the bushes *Williamsoniella* and *Wielandiella*, whose very small, simple, hermaphroditic blossoms could potentially have been pollinated by insects.

Bennettite leaves are very similar to those borne by cycads. They differ only in the cellular structure of their epidermis. Bennettite leaves, like those of the cycads, are usually singly pinnate or else tongue-shaped and with entire edges like *Williamsoniella*.

## Deciphering Dresden's "Raumeria"

The distinguished German palaeobotanist Count H. Solms-Laubach was the first researcher to recognize that the *"Raumeria"* specimen in Dresden is in fact a Bennettite and should be named *Cycadeoidea reichenbachiana*. Both his and Göppert's publications sparked the interest of *Cycadeoidea* specialists in North America. A few years later and after completing some work of his own, Lester Ward decided to visit the Dresden Museum as part of his travels in Europe. Arriving there in 1903, Ward presented a comprehensive report and quite literally turned the *"Raumeria"* specimen upside down - or rather, downside up. Ward saw that, like an Indian fakir, the specimen had been standing on its head for 150 years. In 1911, J. Schuster published a survey of all that was then known about the Dresden trunk and urged specialists to conduct further research on the specimen. Three years earlier, during his own visit to Dresden, Wieland had examined the specimen and likewise urged that it subjected to closer study. After Richard Kräusel, a young palaeobotanist from Frankfurt who had studied in Breslau with Pax (one of Göppert's students), strongly urged that Wieland be permitted to analyze the specimen, the curators of the museum finally agreed to saw a wedge from the trunk and allow Wieland to study the segment. Wieland further dissected the wedge into a large number of thin sections and, in an exchange of letters that continued for ten full years, he repeatedly and enthusiastically praised the extraordinarily well-preserved condition of the Dresden fossil. After lengthy negotiations, Wieland's thin sections were finally returned to Dresden in 1934; they are currently kept there at the Museum for Mineralogy and Geology.

Ill. 7.5
Jurassic *Cycadeoidea sp.*, slice of trunk with central wood surrounded by leaf bases, Patagonia, Argentina

Ill. 7.11 Jurassic *Pentoxylon sp.*, cross-section of a trunk showing 7 wood bodies, Miles (Queensland), Australia.

# Pentoxylon from Gondwana

### Friedemann Schaarschmidt

At the close of the Palaeozoic, our modern continents were fused together into two enormous blocks. To the north, near the Equator, lay the protocontinent of Laurasia which, during the Mesozoic, would eventually break up to yield the continental blocks of North America, Europe and Asia. To the south, near the South Pole, lay the protocontinent of Gondwana which would subsequently separate into the tectonic plates that now bear southern Africa, India, South America and Antarctica. The flora of Laurasia differed markedly from that which flourished on Gondwana. Although these differences would become less distinct during the Mesozoic, certain characteristic differences persisted. One relic which preserves a uniquely Gondwanan feature can be seen in a type of silicified wood that has thus far been found only in Jurassic strata from this southern protocontinent. These specimens were aptly named *Pentoxylon* ("five-wood") by the Indian scientist Srivastava in 1935, who noted that their trunks did not display the typical construction from a single, unified mass of wood, but were composed instead of 5 or 6 (in Australia sometimes more) wood bodies. All of these bodies were embedded within a bark-like tissue, but each wood body had its own growth zones and was able to expand in girth independently of the others.

Since one generally does not find the remains of leaf-bearing lateral twigs on specimens of petrified wood, it is difficult to imagine exactly how *Pentoxylon* actually grew. Scientists believe that it may have been a shrub or small tree with long, non-pinnate, short-stalked leaves. Reproduction took place with the help of small cones measuring a few inches in length.

Where the Pentoxylales actually belong in the phylogenetic system is still unclear. They seem to combine characteristics found among conifers, cycadophytes and ginkgophytes. Perhaps they represent a line of evolution that began with the Palaeozoic *Medullosas* and ended during the Jurassic.

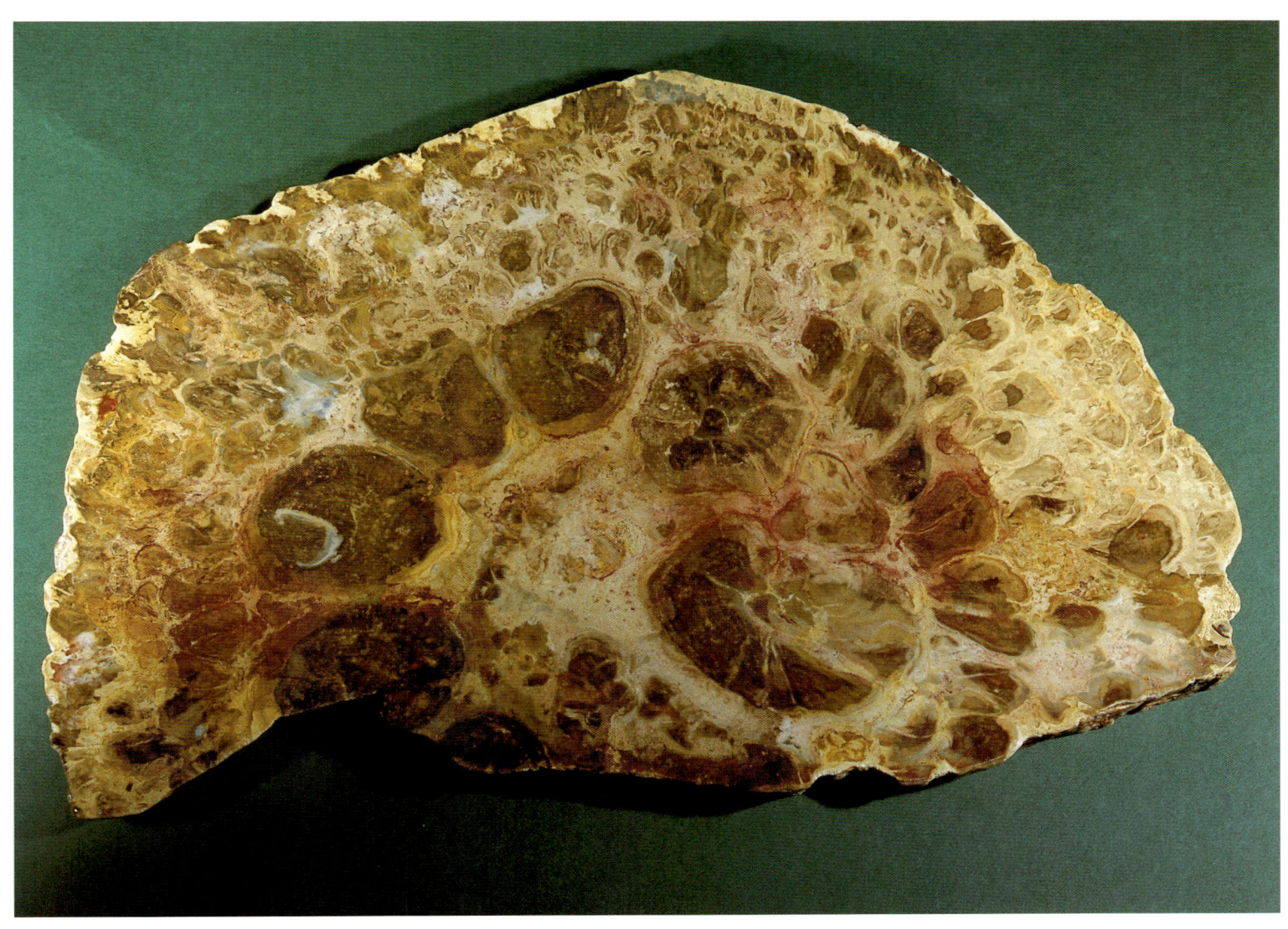

Ill. 7.12 Jurassic *Pentoxylon sp.*, cross-section of an incompletely preserved trunk showing numerous woody bodies, Miles (Queensland), Australia.

# The Araucarias - Wanderers Between North and South

Walter Jung

Andrews, the American palaeobotanist, described *Araucaria heterophylla*, our familiar house or Norfolk Island pine, as a "rather common household article." Two possible reasons might be proposed as explanations for this popularity. First, certain remarkable features about araucarias may have captured the interest of palaeontologists, and second, at least a few types of araucarias (which are named after the Araucanos, a tribe of South American Indians) may be well-known to lay-people. Both suppositions are correct.

Ill. 8.1 Twig from a Lower Permian *Walchia piniformis*, Germany, State Collection, Munich. Photo: F. Höck

Ill. 8.2 Twig from an Upper Jurassic *Agathis jurassica*, Australia, State Collection, Munich. Photo: F. Höck

## Present-Day Distribution

Biologists are fascinated by the distribution and history of this needle-bearing tree. Scientists distinguish at least 20 extant species, all of which are now found only in the southern hemisphere. Two of these occur in South America, the remaining 18 in Australia, New Guinea and above all on the tiny islands in the Pacific. Their ranges of distribution are severely limited. Humankind is partly responsible, since the slender and often perfectly vertical trunks of these trees provide valuable timber, but it seems that the araucarias' range has been diminishing naturally over the past several million years. There are eight endemic araucarias in New Caledonia alone. It is therefore quite appropriate that the so-called "Wollemi pine," which was first discovered in August 1994 and which is represented by a population of only a few dozen individual trees growing in a ravine west of Sydney, appears to belong within the araucaria clan. Since this tree may possibly be closely related to the araucarioid *Agathis jurassica* of the Jurassic (ill. 8.2), popular periodicals were perhaps justified in celebrating it as "a living fossil from the age of the dinosaurs."

## Relatives and Non-relatives

With a few necessary changes, the epithet "living fossil" can be applied to all current members of the araucaria family. Their history stretches a long way back, perhaps as far as the Palaeozoic era some 300 million years ago. The first needle-bearing trees enter the fossil record during the late Carboniferous. Their appearance is quite similar to that of our contemporary "ornamental pine," to use yet another name by which this species of araucaria is sometimes known. Precise study of fossil relics has shown that Palaeozoic *Lebachia* and *Walchia* are not closely related to our araucarias; this distinction should instead be reserved for *Ullmannia*. Though not appreciably more recent than *Lebachia* and *Walchia*, (ill. 8.1) *Ullmannia* evolved single-seeded cone scales and polymorphous needles, just like our contemporary araucarias. Polymorphous needles are a characteristic of many archaic needle-bearing trees. For this reason, our familiar house pine (like another needle-bearing tree of the early Triassic) bears the scientific species name heterophylla, a Greek adjective which means "with heterogeneous leaves." The *heterophylly* of present-day araucarias can be interpreted as a primordial trait inherited from their Jurassic ancestors.

Ill. 8.3 Twig from a Middle Triassic *Voltzia recubariensis*, Italy, State Collection, Munich. Photo: F. Höck

Ill. 8.4 Petrified coniferous wood from a Middle or Upper Jurassic *Araucarioxylon*, Argentina

Certainty about the relationships between the conifers ("cone-bearers") can only be achieved by understanding the construction of their cones, which are in fact the fruit bodies of coniferous trees. Yet it is here that a yawning gap in the fossil record separates the Permian period (from which various species of *Ullmannia* have been recovered) from the more recent Jurassic period. Early Mesozoic fossils of conifer twigs have been recovered from many sites, and the remains of some cones have also been found. Older literature generally assigns the name *Araucarites* to these twigs and cones, but more recent scholarship has determined that most of these specimens came from other conifers, e.g., from trees belonging to the once widely distributed *Voltzia* group. Although many specimens of Mesozoic woods exhibit araucarioid construction akin to that found in today's araucarias, it would seem that many other genera of Triassic conifer trees likewise employed a similar structure, so that even if a specimen deserves to bear the form-genus name *Araucarioxylon*, it needn't necessarily represent a petrified piece of wood from an araucaria tree. On the other hand, twigs discovered in England and variously known as *Brachyphyllum* or *Pagiophyllum* surely bore araucaria cones, although there is also equally reliable fossil evidence that boughs from other trees (e.g., *Hirmerella* or *Voltzia*, ill. 8.3) were clad with similarly thick coats of close-lying scaly needles.

To render the confusion complete, Palaeozoic woods assigned to the form-genus *Dadoxylon* are in fact derived from widely different groups of gymnosperms such as *Cordaites, Walchia, Ullmannia, Pteridosperms*, etc., all of which had already evolved araucarioid characteristics. For this reason, palaeobotanists have traditionally adopted the simple expedient of naming all Palaeozoic woods *Dadoxylon* and all Mesozoic woods *Araucarioxylon* (ill. 8.4) Since this procedure is neither scientifically satisfactory nor nomenclaturally rigorous, some researchers include all woods with araucarioid structure within the form-genus *Dadoxylon* (ill. 8.5). Regardless of its merits or lack thereof, their suggestion has not been widely accepted.

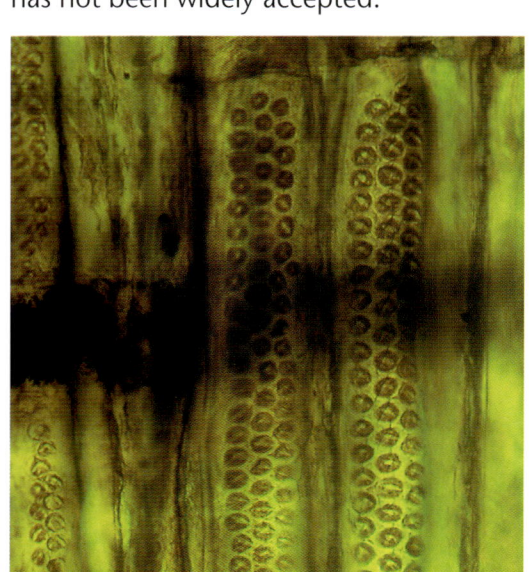

Ill. 8.5 Radial section from an Upper Triassic *Dadoxylon orbiculatum*, Germany, State Collection, Munich. Photo: A. Selmeier

Identification can be made with relative certainty whenever well-preserved cones or cone parts are present. It is by virtue of the distinctive structure of its cones that the araucaria family most clearly asserts its claim to independent stature. The basic structure of araucaria cones conforms to the regularity first recognized by the Swedish scientist Florin. Araucaria cones are built from so-called "double-scale complexes," each of which involves a single bract positioned atop a single seed-scale. These complexes are attached spirally along the cone's woody axis (ill. 8.6). Unlike other conifers, araucarias have large and prominent bracts, with seed-scales reduced to small, inconspicuous ovuliferous scales or "ligula." Since modern araucaria cones fall apart when ripe, and since it can be assumed that this deciduousness was also the case among archaic araucarias, it is not surprising to note that the fossil record has yielded a great many discoveries of isolated individual scales, each of which bore only a single seed (ill. 8.7). Although relics of archaic araucaria cones have been found in many places (including England, continental Europe, India, North and South America, Australia, Antarctica, New Zealand, South Africa, and most recently also in Japan), nowhere is their state of preservation, aesthetic appeal, and abundance greater

Ill. 8.6 Cone and twig from *Araucaria heterophylla*

Ill. 8.6 Cone axis from a Middle or Upper Jurassic *Araucaria mirabilis,* Argentina

Ill. 8.7 Cone scale from an Upper Jurassic *Araucaria haeberleinii*, Germany, State Collection. Photo: F. Höck

Ill. 8.8 Male, pollen-bearing cone from a Middle or Upper Jurassic *Araucaria mirabilis*, Argentina.

than in Cerro Cuadrado Petrified Forest in Patagonia (ill. 8.9). These petrifications are so well preserved that scientists have been able to examine even the tiniest details in the construction of cones and ovules. Spegazzini was so impressed with these specimens that he gave them the flattering species name *mirabilis*, Latin for "wonderful." Fossils of pollen-bearing male cones are extremely rare (ill. 8.8). A difficult situation is worsened by the fact that most of these male cones are poorly preserved. This is understandable when one considers that pollen-producing inflorescences are usually short lived. Because they begin to decay soon after producing pollen, only a very brief time period is available for their potential preservation. Fossilization would have to occur after their production by the plant and before their subsequent decay. Despite these unfavorable circumstances, a few such fossils have in fact formed and been found, for example in Patagonia and in English Jurassic sediments.

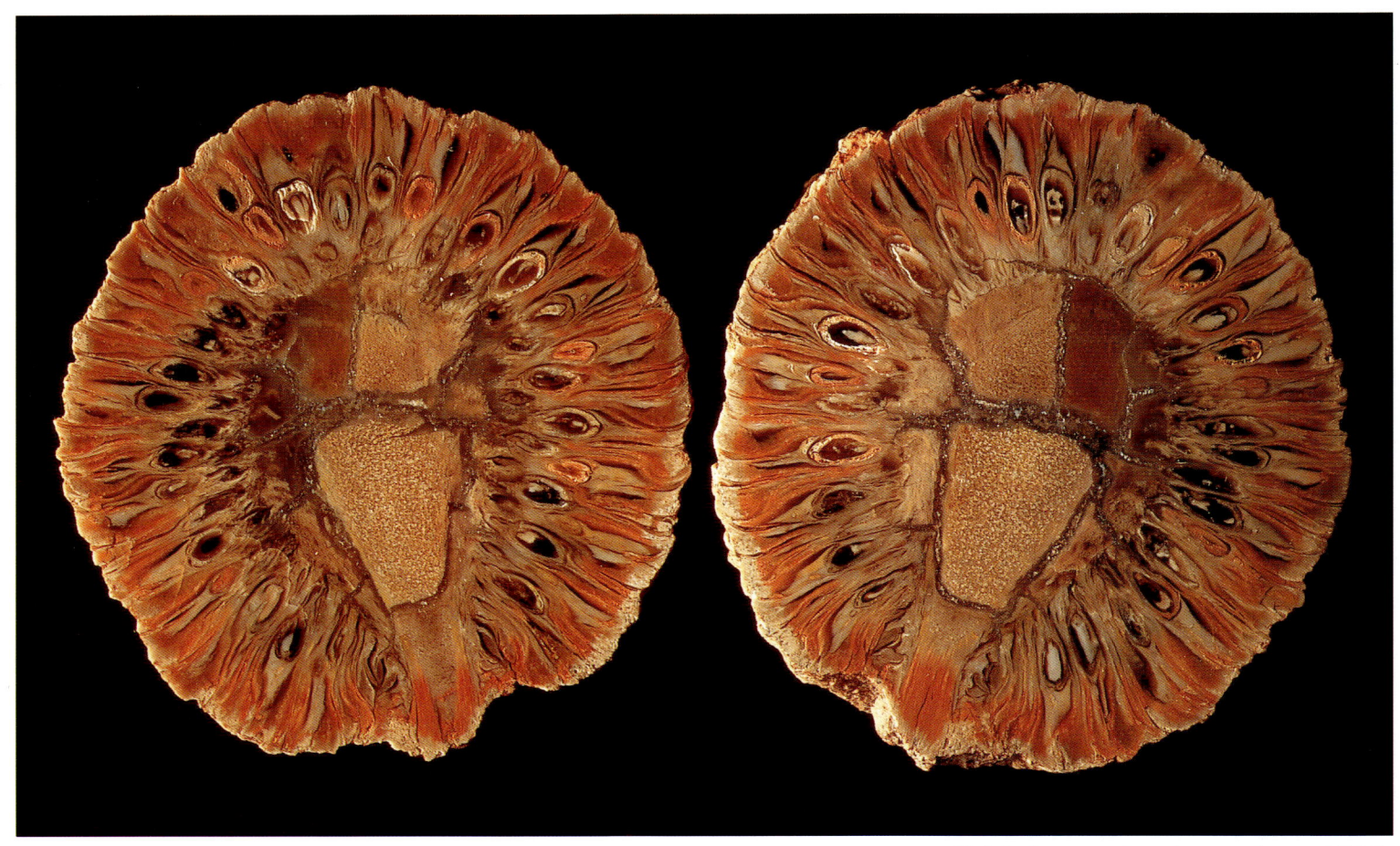

Ill. 8.9 Cross-section of a cone from a Middle or Upper Jurassic *Araucaria mirabilis*, Argentina

**Ill. 8.10**
*Araucaria aruacana*,
twig with cone

**Ill. 8.11**
Twig from a Lower Tertiary *Doliostrobus taxiformis*,
Austria, State Collection, Munich. Photo: F. Höck.

# Tertiary Retreat - Current Range

Although present-day araucarias grow wild only in the southern hemisphere, a glance at the list of sites where araucaria fossils have been found reveals that during the Late Jurassic and Early Cretaceous eras (when the araucarias enjoyed their widest distribution), they must have flourished in the northern as well as the southern hemisphere. European araucarias apparently belonged to a group which included our familiar house or Norfolk Island pine as well as several other species. The sides of the bracts on their cones are drawn outward into wing-like extensions; this helps in their wind dispersion. Araucarias probably vanished from the northern hemisphere by the early Tertiary; araucaria remains from Tertiary and post-Tertiary sediments have been found only within the genus' current range. Relics of twigs and cone-scales from *Doliostrobus*, which deserves to be classed among the araucarias' distant relatives, have been found in Europe. *Doliostrobus*, which bore branches whose needles bent forwards along its twigs, reminds one of an araucaria. This similarity prompted earlier palaeobotanists to assign it the name *Araucarites*. Like araucaria cones, *Doliostrobus* cones also fall apart upon maturity (ill. 8.11).

Andrews' observation that the house pine has become a "rather common household article" emphasizes that araucarias are re-inhabiting their primeval homelands. This return to their former range applies not only to the Norfolk Island pine (*A. heterophylla*) that James Cook discovered in 1774, but also to other species of araucaria which are presently cultivated either indoors or, where climates are sufficiently mild, in gardens and parks throughout the northern hemisphere. Gardeners are fond of the primitive-looking Andes or Chile pine (*A. araucana*, ill. 8.10) with its thorn-like, scaly leaves. Another popular araucaria is the Bunya pine (*A. bidwillii*) of the Australian Aborigines. Its cones display some archaic features. The Bunya pine is related to *Araucaria mirabilis* of Cerro Cuadrado. The Norfolk Island pine was first cultivated in 1793; the Andes pine in 1795; and the Bunya pine in 1843. Starting around the mid-19th century and spreading from their newly recovered English homeland, all three species began a worldwide horticultural victory march - as wanderers between north and south.

Ill. 9.1 Leaves from a Middle Jurassic *Ginkgo huttonii,* Germany, State Collection, Munich. Photo: F. Höck.

# The Ginkgo - Forever Green

## Walter Jung

Quite a few so-called "living fossils" have been discovered in both the animal and plant kingdoms. But neither the mammoth sequoia tree nor the ancient cycads, the sphenodon lizards nor the chambered nautilus, indeed, not even the bizarre tassel-finned *Latimeria* fish have been as lavishly celebrated in scientific and belletristic literature as the fabled ginkgo tree. This remarkable plant is variously known to Germans as the *Fächerblattbaum* (fan-leaf tree), to the English-speaking world as the maidenhair tree, to Francophones as *l'arbre aux quarante écus,* to the Japanese as the *icho,* and to the Chinese as the *yin hsing.*

Botanists, pharmacologists and apothecaries, poets, artists and gardeners have all been fascinated by the ginkgo. Admiration for this extraordinary tree increased still further, and its reputation experienced yet another boost, when one specimen of this hardy arboreal race survived the catastrophic nuclear blast that destroyed Hiroshima in August 1945: although it stood a mere 2,460 feet (800 m) from the center of the explosion, the tree sprouted fresh leaves the following spring! The following article will emphasize the plant's palaeobotanical aspects, but will not entirely ignore some other interesting facts about this unique tree.

Ill. 9.2  Twig with forked leaves from a Lower Permian; *Dicranophyllum gallicum,* France, State Collection, Munich. Photo: F. Höck.

## A Tree With a Long History

Charles Darwin popularized the phrase "living fossil." The epithet well suits the ginkgo and its relatives, since they can indeed look back upon a long history. The origins of the ginkgo family are lost in the obscure depths of the Palaeozoic era. Possible ancestors of the ginkgo include: *Ginkgophytopsis* (or *Ginkgophyton*), whose 11.75-inch (30-cm) long, undivided, inverted cuneiform leaves have been preserved as 330-million-year-old fossils from the Middle Carboniferous; and *Dicranophyllum* (ill. 9.2), a tree-like plant with small, multiply forked leaves that flourished some 290 million years ago during the transitional years between the Carboniferous and Permian periods. The relationship between the modern ginkgo and the Upper Devonian *Eddya* of North America with its inverted cuneiform, 2.4-inch (6-cm) long leaves is unclear. For many years, most palaeobotanists agreed that the Lower Permian *Trichopitys* was the oldest certain relative of today's ginkgo. More recently *Trichopitys* has been obliged to share that honor with the equally ancient Argentinean genus *Polyspermophyllum* and other candidates among the taxonomically problematic, Palaeozoic leaf types known as *Ginkgoites, Ginkgophyllum* and *Ginkgoidium.* The debate continues, but most specialists agree that the roots of the ginkgo family tree are probably to be found among the progymnosperms, most likely in the vicinity of *Aneurophyton* and *Archaeopteris.* The ginkgo's phylogenetic tree trunk must have branched into several different boughs at an early date. Unfortunately, most of the subsequent forms are known only from leaf fossils. Fruits or blossoms are rare. The leaves present a great diversity of forms from linguiform undivided (*Glossophyllum*) to forked weakly divided to forked severely slit (*Baiera,* ill. 9.3). Among this plethora of forms, the ancient plants that bore stalked leaves with moderately broad forked lobes (originally described as *Ginkgoites,* but with increasing frequency simply called *Ginkgo,* ill. 9.1) probably deserve a place in the direct ancestral lineage leading to our modern *Ginkgo biloba.* Leaves of this sort are first bond in strata between the Triassic and Jurassic periods (ill. 9.4), i.e., in sediments

Ill. 9.3  Leaf from a Lower Jurassic *Baiera muensteriana,* Germany, State Collection, Munich. Photo: F. Höck.

deposited 200 million years ago. Mesozoic sediments have yielded many ginkgo types. One palaeobotanist (Daber) counted between 120 and 150 different species, although he did not distinguish between *Ginkgo, Ginkgoites, Baiera* and *Salisburia.* This number is sure

Ill. 9.4 Leaf from a Lower Jurassic *Ginkgo taeniata*, Germany, State Collection, Munich. Photo: F. Höck.

to shrink as research methods improve and as existing or newly discovered fossil material is scrutinized under the microscope. The ginkgo clan's diversity must have peaked during the Jurassic or Cretaceous, when ginkgo-like trees appeared in the southern hemisphere. Along with seed ferns, horsetails and conifers, the presence of ginkgos south of the Equator provides yet another proof of the intimate north-south link that existed among the flora of that period.

Most experts agree that by the Tertiary only a single type of ginkgo (*Ginkgo adiantoides*) still survived, although its fossils have been found in a variety of shapes. Other scientists claim that two forms survived. The species name *adiantoides* is particularly well chosen, since even the botanist Kaempfer (who introduced the modern ginkgo to the Western world - see page 179) had called attention to the similarity between the leaves of the modern ginkgo and the delicate fronds of the maidenhair fern *Adiantum*.

The forms of the leaves preserved in Tertiary fossils are scarcely different from the leaves that sprout each spring on the twigs of our *Ginkgo biloba*. The ginkgo clan's decline continued during the Tertiary. The ginkgo was still widely distributed during the Early and Middle Tertiary in North America (ill. 9.5), across Greenland, into Scotland and Spitzbergen, and onward through Siberia into China and Japan, but by the end of the Tertiary its range had dwindled to a few isolated forests in Europe and groves in Japan and China. With the exception of what seem to be endemic populations thriving in the mountain forests of southeastern China, our Quarternary period has seen ginkgo trees surviving only in cultivation, although its hardiness and popularity have contributed to its reintroduction throughout the world. With a little help from *Homo sapiens*, *Ginkgo biloba* has reconquered its original Mesozoic range.

# Western Science Discovers the Ginkgo

It was physician, botanist and world traveler Engelbert Kaempfer who first brought the ginkgo to the attention of Western botanists shortly after he discovered it in Japan in 1691. Volume five of Kaempfer's book *Amoenitatum exoticarum politico-physico-medicarum fasciculi V* (1712) includes a sketch and Latin description of the tree. In his transcription of the Sino-Japanese ideogram, Kaempfer spelled the tree's name with a penultimate "g" rather than with a "y" or "j". Not "ginkgo," but "ginkyo" or "ginkjo" would have been the correct transcription of the ideogram, which translates into English as "silver apricot." Linné unknowingly preserved Kaempfer's error when he applied his binomial nomenclature to this tree in 1771. Despite the mistake, international nomenclature has kept this traditional spelling for the tree that first caught

Ill. 9.5 Leaf from a Lower Tertiary *Ginkgo adiantoides*, USA, State Collection, Munich. Photo: F. Höck.

Kaempfer's eye in the late 17th century. Recognition of Kaempfer's and Linné's error would spark heated discussions, and some botanists even recommended renaming the genus as *Salisburia*. Although new to Europeans, it would be foolishly Eurocentric to pretend that the ginkgo had not been well-known in Japan (ill. 9.6) for centuries. Some Japanese temple gardens feature venerable specimens whose ages have been estimated at as much as 1,000 years. In China, where the tree is known as *ya chio* or *yin hsing*, it is first mentioned in documents dating from the late 10th or early 11th century. Both the Chinese and the Japanese knew that the tree's nut-like seeds were edible and that the plant had medicinal value. The assertion that the oldest Chinese ginkgo trees are 4,000 years old is surely an exaggeration.

How to spell "ginkgo" is one problem, but the tree also confronts botanists with several other conundrums. Where does this exotic oriental tree really belong in the tidy taxonomy of the plant kingdom? Linné was loathe to commit himself, and his disciple Thunberg placed the ginkgo with the so-called *plantae obscurae,* i.e., among the botanical oddities. The ginkgo is a peculiar plant in many respects. Most obvious is the unusual shape of its leaves, but it also exhibits several other oddities: its female inflorescence does not look at all like a cone; it alternately bears long and short sprouts; its male germ cells (spermatozoids) are mobile, ciliate, and of comparatively gigantic size (up to 0.1 mm); and a lag of up to several months may separate pollination from fertilization, so that in some cases seeds may fall from the tree and undergo dispersal while still unfertilized. All of these peculiarities are reasons why *Ginkgo biloba* has been regarded as the sole survivor of a separate class of plants, the Ginkgoatae or Ginkgoopsida, which is thought to have evolved as an independent branch of the progymnosperms. Until 1897, however, taxonomists mistakenly classed the ginkgo among the needle-bearing trees, the conifers.

Ill. 9.6 *Ginkgo biloba,* reproduction of plate 136 in: Siebold & Zuccarini, *Flora Japonica*; Leiden 1835/42.

Ill. 9.7 Polished slice of trunk from an Upper Tertiary *Ginkgoxylon beckii*, USA.

Another unexplained problem is the dearth of fossil ginkgo wood. The prehistoric ginkgo and its Mesozoic relatives were woody plants, so one would expect to find a fairly large number of fossilized trunks or twigs. Petrified remains of other trees have been discovered in geological strata of the appropriate age, but petrified ginkgo woods have either not been found at all or have only been unearthed as rare, individual discoveries. One explanation for this scarcity suggests that ginkgo petrifications may have been mistaken for fossils from other trees, especially cypresses. Another explanation posits that ginkgo trunks were highly susceptible to decay. A third theory proposes that Mesozoic ginkgo wood may have had a different anatomical structure from that now seen in modern specimens of *Ginkgo biloba*. In any case, supposed identifications of ginkgo wood in petrified specimens from Hungary, southern Germany and elsewhere are generally regarded with scepticism.

One noteworthy exception is Ginkgo Petrified Forest in the U.S.A., where Miocene sediments have yielded more than 200 species of trees including fir, pine, Douglas fir, sequoia, oak, maple, horse chestnut, hickory, walnut, sycamore, and many other types of trees -- as well as gorgeous petrified trunks of Tertiary ginkgo trees (ill. 9.7). As is the case at other sites where so-called "petrified forests" have been preserved, here in Washington State volcanic activity caused tree trunks to become embedded in masses of lava through which water rich in silicic acid seeped, eventually silicifying (i.e., petrifying) the trunks. Before their interment, flooding rivers swept these trees from their original places of growth in the mountains down to the sites where they are found today. In the millennia following their burial and petrification, natural erosive forces uncovered more and more petrified trunks, removing overlying material and again allowing the light of day to shine upon these ancient trees.

Along with this rare case of the petrification of ginkgo wood, fossils of ginkgo leaves have been found in Tertiary strata at a fairly large number of other sites. More than half a dozen Late Tertiary sites exist in southern Germany alone (ill. 9.8).

## Return to the West

Although it became extinct in Europe during the Late Tertiary, horticultural curiosity returned the ginkgo to the Occident in 1727/30, some 40 years prior to its "scientific birth." Most historians believe that it was first cultivated in Europe at the botanical garden in Utrecht; it was planted in London's Kew Gardens some 25 years later; and the first seedlings were brought to North America in 1784, approximately ten million years after it disappeared from that continent.

ually forced to retreat further south. It is also conceivable that ginkgos in North America and northern Asia were unable to withstand the competition posed by the increasingly more dominant angiosperm flowering plants. This seems all the more astonishing from today's standpoint, especially when one considers that the ginkgo has shown itself to be unusually hardy in the face of adverse environmental conditions. It possesses truly incredible regenerative powers: for example, it is able to sprout from so-called "sleeping eyes," a unique type of dormant bud which the Chinese call *tschi tschi*.

Ill. 9.8
Leaf from an Upper Tertiary *Ginkgo adiantoides*, Germany, State Collection, Munich. Photo: F. Höck.

The ginkgo's demise in Europe was mostly due to climatic changes associated with the Ice Age. The cherry-sized, apricot-colored seed of the ginkgo is a reproductive organ which relies on animals for its dispersal. When the tree was compelled to alternate between retreat from approaching ice masses and attempts at recolonization during warmer interglacial periods, the ginkgo's large seeds were simply too ponderous. Inclement climate elsewhere in the world may also have contributed to the plant's Tertiary decline. Fossil relics prove that the ginkgo was present in the belt of mixed deciduous forests that had advanced into rather high northern latitudes by the Early Tertiary. But as the Earth's climate became progressively cooler, these forests were grad-

Today, the ginkgo tree numbers among the best-loved species of plants cultivated along roads and in parks. This popularity is not solely due to its ability to flourish despite severe concentrations of smoke and automobile exhaust. Gingkos account for approximately 2% of the trees planted along roads in the U.S.A.

When one ponders its botanical uniqueness, its ecological tenacity, its fascinating past, its significance in pharmacology and the arts (two fields which we have not discussed here), and its literary fame (primarily due to Goethe's well-known poem) , one must admit that the ginkgo truly is one of our planet's most remarkable life forms.

# Bibliography

**In Chapters 1 + 4 (Selmeier)**

Barefoot, A. C. & Hankins, F. W. (1982):
Identification of modern and Tertiary woods. 189 p.; Oxford (Clarendon Press).

Grosser, D. (1977):
Die Hölzer Mitteleuropas. Ein mikrophotographischer Lehratlas. - 288 p.; Berlin etc. (Springer).

IAWA Committee (1989):
IAWA list of microscopic features for hardwood identification. - IAWA Bull, n. p., 10: 219 - 232; Leiden (Rijksherbarium).

Ilic, J. (1991):
CSIRO Atlas of Hardwoods. - 525 p.; Berlin etc. (Springer).

Kräusel, R. (1939):
Ergebnisse der Forschungsreisen Prof. E. Stromer's in den Wüsten Ägyptens, IV. Die fossilen Floren Ägyptens. - Abh. bayer. Akad. Wiss., math.-naturwiss. Abt., N.F., 47: 1 - 140; München.

Mädel, E. (1962):
Die fossilen Euphorbiaceen-Hölzer mit besonderer Berücksichtigung neuer Funde aus der Oberkreide Süd-Afrikas. - Senck. leth., 43: 283 - 321; Frankfurt a. M.

Salard, M. (1962):
Contribution a la connaissance del la flore fossile de la Nouvell Caledonie. - Palaeontographica, B. 124: 1 - 44; Stuttgart.

Schönfeld, G. (1947):
Hölzer aus dem Tertiär von Kolumbien. - Abh. senck. naturf. Ges., 475: 1-53; Frankfurt a. M.

Schweingruber, F. H. (1990):
Atlas mitteleuropäischer Hölzer. - 802 S.; Bern u. Stuttgart (P. Haupt).

Suzuki, M. & Watari, S. (1994):
Fossil Wood Flora of the Early Miocene Nawamata Formation of Monzen, Noto Peninsula, Central Japan. - J. Plant Research, 107: 63 - 76; Tokyo.

Taylor, N. T. & Taylor, E. L. (1993):
The Biology and Evolution of Fossil Plants. - 982 p.; New Jersy, USA (Englewood Clioffs).

Wheeler, E. A. & Baas, P. (1991):
A survey of the fossil record for dicotyledonous wood and its significance for evolutionary and ecological wood anatomy. - IAWA Bull., n.p., 12: 275 - 332; Leiden (Rijksherbarium).

**In Chapters 6, 8 + 9 (Jung):**

Andrews, H. N. (1947):
Ancient plants and the world they lived in. - 188 p.; Ithaca & London (Cornell Univ. Press).

Andrews, H. N. (1980):
The fossil hunters. - 421 p.; Ithaca & London (Cornell Univ. Press).

Jung, W. (1994):
Wälder aus Stein und Kohle. - Extra Lapis, 7: 24-31; München.

Jung, W., Selmeier, A. & Dernbach, U. (1992):
Araucaria. - 160 p.; Lorsch (D´Oro).

Melzheimer, V. (1992):
Ginkgo biloba L., aus der Sicht der systematischen und angewandten Botanik. - Pharmazie in unserer Zeit, 21: 206-214; Weinheim.

Michel, P.-F. (1986): Ginkgo biloba. - 168 p.; Paris (L´Art du vivant - Éditions du Félin).

Müller, I (1992):
Zur Einführung des Ginkgo biloba in die europäische Botanik und Pharmazie. - Pharmazie in unserer Zeit, 21: 201-205; Weinheim.

Schmid, M. & Schmoll, H. gen. Eisenwerth (1994):
Ginkgo. - 135 S.; Stuttgart (Wissenschaftl. VerlagsgmbH).

Sterzel, J. T. & Weber, O. (1869):
Beiträge zur Kenntnis der Medulloseae. - Ber. Naturwiss. Ges. Chemnitz, 13: 44-143; Chemnitz.

**In Chapters 7 (Schaarschmidt):**

Goeppert, H. R. 1853:
Über die gegenwärtigen Verhältnisse der Paläontologie in Schlesien sowie über fossile Cycadeen. — Jubiläums-Denkschrift Schles. Ges. Vaterländ. Kultur; Breslau.

Kräusel, R. 1925:
Raumeria Reichenbachiana und ihre Verwandten, ausgestorbene Cycadophyten des Mesozoikums. — Aus Natur und Museum, 1925: 310-316, 6 Abb., Frankfurt am Main.

Schuster, J. 1911:
Über Goepperts Raumeria im Zwinger zu Dresden. — Sitzungsber. Königl. Bayer. Akad. Wiss., Math.-physik. Klasse, Jg. 1911: 489-504, 3 Taf., 5 Abb.; München.

Solms-Laubach, H. 1887:
Einleitung in die Paläophytologie vom botanischen Standpunkt aus. — 416 S., 49 Abb.; Leipzig. (Felix).

Walther, H. 1988: Die Paläontologische Sammlung. In: Mathé, G. (Hrsg.): Staatliches Museum für Mineralogie und Geologie Dresden. — S. 23-34, Abb. 22-35; Dresden.

Wieland, G. R. 1906:
American fossil Cycads. — Vol. 1; Washington D.C. (Carnegie Insitute)

Wieland, G. R. 1916:
American fossil Cycads. — Vol. 2; Washington D.C. (Carnegie Insitute)

# Glossary

**adventitious roots** (Lat. *advenire* - to come toward) renewed division of cells near the vascular bundle's phloem can cause lateral rooting along the shoot axis

**Angiospermae** (Gr. *angeion* - vessel; *sperma* - seed) seed formation in these plants occurs within the fruit node; antonym, see Gymnospermae "naked seeds"

**annual ring** boundary between periodically active cambium during one growth period; boundary between the late wood and the early wood

**araucarioid or araucaroid** (Gr. suffix *-oides* - similar to) araucarioid pitting is a special form of bordered pitting; it occurs today only among members of the Araucariaceae clan

**binary nomenclature** system of two-part names used in biology; each species of animal or plant is assigned a two-part scientific name; the first word denotes the organism's genus, the second word denotes its species, e.g., *Ginkgo biloba*

**bordered pits** openings in the cell wall to facilitate exchange of water and nutrients with neighboring cells

**cambium** (Lat. *cambire* - to change) layer of cells capable of dividing; causes secondary thickening; a closed ring, visible in cross-section of the shoot axis, creates "wood" toward the inside and bast toward the outside

**carinal cavities** air-filled, vertically oriented passageways found in horsetails and calamites

**caulinary bundle** (Gr. *kaulos* - stalk) vascular bundle belonging to the stalk itself and leaving no leaf trace

**Cenozoic** (adj.) refers to fossils dating from the Cenozoic era

**Cenozoic era** (Gr. invented word) most recent era of the Earth's history, includes the Tertiary and Quarternary

**coal balls** Carboniferous turf dolomite; rounded, concentric concretions in coal sediments with well-preserved plant remains

**collateral vascular bundle** (Lat. *collateralis* - side by side) most common type of vascular bundle; the woody part is oriented toward the inner portion of the sprout, the phloem is oriented toward the outer portion

**Coniferae** (Lat. *conus* - cone, *ferre* - to bear) a group of gymnosperms which includes our familiar needle-bearing trees

**cormus** (Gr. *kormos* - trunk, sprout) plant body composed of the sprout axis, root and leaves; antonym is the thallus

**denudation** the entirety of all processes leading toward widespread transport of eroded materials

**early wood** formed at the beginning of the annual growth cycle; in needle-bearing trees, early wood is recognizable as the paler portion of each annual ring; wide-lumened early-wood tracheids serve to transport water and nutrients

**endarchic protoxylem** the small-celled, thin-walled protoxylem lies within, the thicker-walled metaxylem adjoins it toward the outside along the periphery of the trunk

**endemic** restriction of a plant group (family, genus or species) to an isolated and spatially delimited area

**etymological** (adj.) refers to etymology, denotes that subdivision of linguistics which attempts to provide historical explanations for the formation of words

**eustele** (Gr. *eu* - well, *stele* - column, trunk) central cylinder with ring-shaped arrangement of vascular bundles

**evolution** the study of descent of species; evolution postulates that living beings are descended from primordial forms in accord with a natural sequence of development

**exarchic protoxylem** the small-celled, thin-walled protoxylem lies on the outside, the thick-walled metaxylem adjoins it toward the center of the trunk

**form genus** established for reasons of practicality to describe fossils which lack other characteristics needed to determine the identities of their natural relatives

**fossil** (Lat. *fossa* - ditch, trench) term used to describe the remains of organisms preserved from ancient geological eras

**frond** stalked, richly veined, large leaves (megaphylle) typical of Pteridopsida (ferns) and Cycadopsida ("palm ferns")

**Gymnospermae** (Gr. *gymnos* - naked, *sperma* - seed) in "naked seeders," unlike Angiosperamae, the ovaries are freely accessible to the pollinating pollen grain

**habit** (Lat. *habitus* - state, dress) the design and appearance of a plant or fossil

**heart wood** inner part of the woody body with dead cells that are no longer involved in water transport; antonym is known as sapwood or alburnum

**heterophylly** in the course of a plant's growth, the development of variously shaped leaves, having various life expectancies and functions

**late wood** formed at the end of the annual growth cycle; in needle-bearing trees, late wood is recognizable as the darker portion of each annual ring; narrow-lumened late-wood tracheids provide structural support

**leaf base** the base of the leaf which remains on the plant after the leaf has fallen off

**leaf trace** the entirety of the vascular bundles leading from the shoot axis into the leaf

**ligua** a triangular membrane with a sunken basis found near the leaf cushion in lycopod-like plants

**medullary rays** narrow, radially oriented bands of cells which support the radial distribution of materials from the bark to the pith; formerly known as pith rays

**meristele vascular bundle** part of the leaf trace strand, its arrangement and structure are visible in cross-sections of the sprout

**mesarchic protoxylem** (Gr. *mesos* - in the middle, *arche* -beginning, *protos* - the first, *xylem* - wood) the small-celled, thin-walled protoxylem lies in the middle; the thick-walled metaxylem surrounds the protoxylem

**Mesozoic** (adj.) refers to fossils dating from the Mesozoic era

**Mesozoic era** (Gr. invented word) ntermediate era of the Earth's history, includes the Triassic, Jurassic and Cretaceous

**metaxylem** the small-celled, thin-walled tracheids of the protoxylem develop into thicker-walled, adjacent metaxylem

**morphological genus** ➜ form genus

**Nautilus** a genus of cephalopods with variously shaped outer shells; only a few species survive today; formerly included many species and enjoyed worldwide distribution

**Occident** (Lat. *occidens* - setting) the West, as contrasted with the East or Orient

**palaeobotany** (Gr. *palaeos* - old, *botane* - grass, fodder) a subdivision of biology that deals with the remains of plants from past periods of the Earth's geological history

**palaeoxylotomy** (Gr. *palaeos* - old, *xylon* - wood) the study of the construction of fossilized woody remains; research is conducted using thin sections

**Palaeozoic** (adj.) refers to fossils dating from the Palaeozoic era

**Palaeozoic era** (Gr. invented word) earliest era of the Earth's history, includes Cambrian, Ordovician, Silurian, Carboniferous and Permian

**parenchyma** (Gr. *para* - beside, *enchyma* - infusion) thin-walled basic tissue of plants

**pinna** individual lateral leaflets arranged in a featherlike manner along the axis of a fern, seed-fern or palm-fern frond

**Progymnospermae** palaeozoic woody plants with secondary thickening and terminally arranged, thick-walled sporangia; the ancestors of the Gymnospermae

**protoxylem** the first type of vascular element; small-celled, thin-walled wood cells within the sprout axis; more efficient, thicker-walled vascular elements (metaxylem) subsequently took over the function formerly served by the protoxylem

**pycnoxyl** typical cell structure in the secondary wood of the Coniferophytina with densely layered bordered pit tracheids, narrow medullary rays, and devoid of vessels (tracheids)

**radial section** a cut taken longitudinally along the radius of the annual rings toward the center and perpendicular to the tangential section

**radiation** a period of time when an organism expands its range and distribution

**sclerenchyma** (Gr. *skleros* - hard, brittle) dead tissue composed of thick-walled, narrow-lumened cells, the function of sclerenchyma is to provide structural support

**secondary thickening** (Lat. *secundus* - second) formation of additional (secondary) tissue associated with increase in the diameter of a sprout, trunk or root; activity of the cambium is the cause of secondary thickening

**secondary xylem** (Gr. *xylem* - wood) the entirety the wood formed toward the interior of the shoot by the cambium

**sori** groups of spore containers (sporangia), generally found on the undersides of fern fronds

**sporangia** (Gr. *sporos* - to sow, *angeion* - container) a container inside of which spores develop

**stele** (Gr. *stele* - trunk, column) the central cylinder of the sprout axis with all vascular tissue

**synangium** capsule-like, fan-shaped, later dehiscent container filled with sporangia

**tangential section** a cut made parallel to the axis of the trunk as a tangent to the annual rings, also known as a "board" or "flat" cut

**tassel-fins** *Crossopterygii*, a group of fishes known from fossils dating from the Devonian period, rediscovered alive in 1952 near Madagascar off the southeast coast of Africa

**thin section** a slide of 10-50 millionths of meter in thickness, prepared using a stone saw and sanding machine, and cut so thinly as to permit observation under a visible-light microscope

**transcribe** (L. *transcribere* - to transcribe) to write over from one book into another

**xylem** (Gr. *xylon* - wood) woody part; in vascular bundles, the xylem is the water-carrying portion

# The Authors

**Prof. Dr. Rafael Herbst**

Born in Hamburg in 1936. Bachelor's degree, Colegio Nacional, Tucuman in 1953. Studied geology at the University of Tucuman, Ph.D. in 1963. Afterwards assistant in palaeontology, concentration in palaeobotany. Full professorship and permission to teach at the University of Corrientes in 1967. Guest professor in Paraguay until 1977. Since 1983, director of PRINGEPA, Institute for Geology and Palaeontolgy in Corrientes and editor of D'ORBIGNYANA, PRINGEPA's scientific journal. An expert on palm ferns.

**Prof. Dr. Walter Jung**

Born in Nuremberg in 1931. Abitur from secondary school emphasizing classical languages in 1951. Studied natural sciences at Ludwig-Maximilians-University, Munich; specialized in botany, zoology, geography, chemistry and palaeontology for university teachers. Ph.D. under Prof. Mägdefrau in 1959, dissertation in palaeontolgy. Active at the Institute for Palaeontology and Historical Geology of the University of Munich since 1962. Full professorship in palaeobotany in 1967. Extraordinary professorship in 1978.

**Prof. Dr. Friedemann Schaarschmidt**

Born in Pleissa, Saxony in 1934. Secondary school at Limbach-Oberfrohna, abitur in 1952. Studied at Friedrich-Schiller-University in Jena, diploma in biology, minored in geology, in 1957. Director of science department at Meininger Museum in 1957. Scientific collaborator with the state geological commission of the G.D.R. Graduate study at Johann-Wolfgang-Goethe-University in Frankfurt am Main (1960), Ph.D. in biology and geology/palaeontology under Prof. Dr. Richard Kräusel in 1962. Director of palaeobotany at the research institute of Frankfurt University from 1962 to 1966. Professorship and permission to teach palaeontology at Frankfurt University in 1984. Received honorary professorship in 1992.

**Prof. Dr. Alfred Selmeier**

Born in Freising in 1923. Abitur in Munich, 1942. Studied biology, chemistry and geography at Ludwig-Maximilians-University in Munich and at the Technical University in Weihenstephan. Ph.D. in 1959. Scientific collaborator at the Institute for Palaeontology and Historical Geology of the University of Munich. Focus of research: identification of petrified plant remains. Guest researcher at scientific institutions in France, China, the Philippines and the United States.

**Prof. Dr. Evagelos D. Velitzelos**

Born in Vegora, Greece in 1941. Studied geology, botany, chemistry, physics, zoology and palaeontology in Athens. Ph.D. 1972 under Prof. H. Schneider, University of Saarbrücken; dissertation about geology. Scientific collaborator at the Museum for Geology and Palaeontology at Athen's National and Capodistrian University since 1975. Professor for palaeobotany and palaeontology since 1993. Current research project: establishing natural history museums in Lesbos, Lemnos, Thrace and Castoria (Greece).

**Ulrich Dernbach**

Born in Bad Salzschlirf, Hessen, in 1939. Abitur in Lauterbach in 1959. Work-study in pharmacy. Studied chemistry in Berlin, 1961. Joined the Merck Group (pharmaceuticals) in 1965, where he is still employed today. First fascination with fossils and emerging personal interest in palaeontology began in 1970. Special interest and focus of his collection: petrified woods from all over the world, and, ever since his first trip to Argentina, araucaria cones from Patagonia. His first book: *Auraucaria*.

**Kurt Noll**

Born in Grünstadt, Palatinate, in 1929. Studied machine fitting in 1944, subsequently worked as a machine fitter. Has been an enthusiastic photographer since earliest youth. Favorite subjects come from mineralogy, his second hobby.

**Robert Noll**

Born in Grünstadt, Palatinate, in 1961. Studied machine fitting in 1976, subsequently employed by BASF. Active as mechanical engineer with BASF since 1993. Enthusiastic hobby photographer. Interested in palaeontology for more than 20 years.

# ARAUCARIA

Petrified cones and petrified wood of araucarias from Cerro Cuadrado, Argentina

With texts by Ulrich Dernbach, Prof. Dr. Walter Jung and Prof. Dr. Alfred Selmeier; photography by Konrad Götz.

160 pages, large 9.5 x 13.5 inch (24 X 34 cm) format, numerous color illustrations, hardcover, DM 98.—

D'ORO Publishers
D-64646 Heppenheim
ISBN 3-932181-00-X

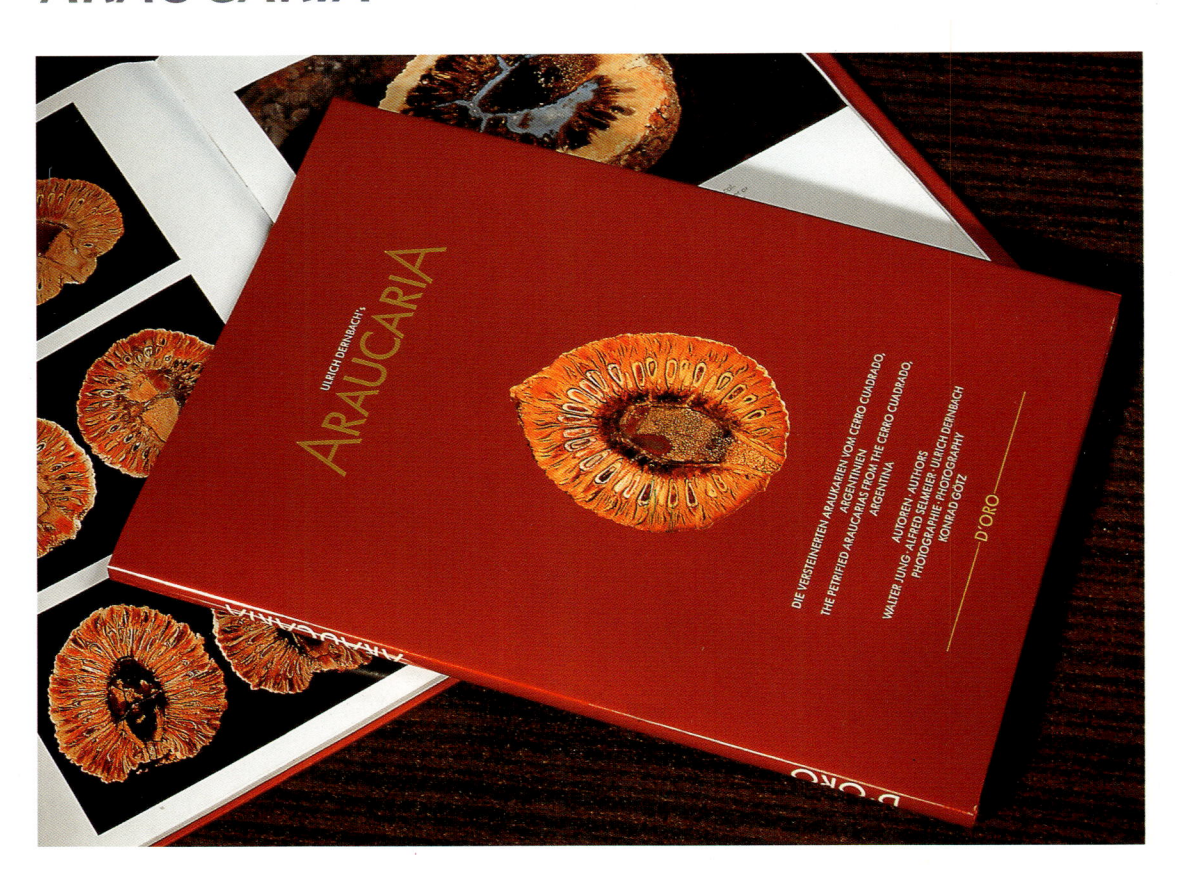

## The Jewel Among the Petrified Forests

The name alone is fascinating: „Araucaria." The very sound of the word evokes the exciting world from which these magnificent trees come. And no less fascinating are the petrified woods from these conifers. The most beautiful specimens come from Arizona and Patagonia, especially the petrified cones that are almost solely found in Cerro Cuadrado, Patagonia, Argentina.

Munich palaeontologist Prof. Dr. Walter Jung, who has been fascinated by araucarias for many years, traces in this book the evolutionary path traversed by the araucarias from their earliest ancestors right down to present-day forms. Particular attention is devoted to the cones of these trees: as if by a miracle, these cones have been petrified at Cerro Cuadrado in a marvelously beautiful and well-preserved state.

An additional portion of the book is devoted to petrified wood. Munich wood anatomist Prof. Dr. Alfred Selmeier studied and identified the fossil woods of Cerro Cuadrado. He also provides a thorough discussion of the delicate structures found in fossilized Patagonian araucaria seedlings.

Ulrich Dernbach wrote the book's introductory chapter. Dernbach, an enthusiastic collector of fossilized woods, has visited the petrified forest at Cerro Cuadrado no fewer than seven times. As an expert on this site, he describes the journey to the remote „Cerro Cuadrado Bosque Petrificado." The photographs that he brought back from his expeditions provide a vivid impression of this fascinating yet severe landscape where the stony hulks of giant petrified trees radiate a special magic all their own.